Richard McAllister Smith

The Confederate first Reader

Containing Selections in Prose and Poetry

Richard McAllister Smith

The Confederate first Reader
Containing Selections in Prose and Poetry

ISBN/EAN: 9783337373139

Printed in Europe, USA, Canada, Australia, Japan

Cover: Foto ©Thomas Meinert / pixelio.de

More available books at **www.hansebooks.com**

THE

CONFEDERATE FIRST READER

CONTAINING

SELECTIONS IN PROSE AND POETRY,

AS READING EXERCISES

FOR THE YOUNGER CHILDREN

IN THE

SCHOOLS AND FAMILIES

OF THE CONFEDERATE STATES.

———◦◦◦◦———

RICHMOND, VA.
PUBLISHED BY G. L. BIDGOOD,
No. 121, Main Street.
1864.

AYRES & WADE, PRINTERS.

PREFACE.

This book has been compiled and prepared for the use of children who may have mastered the reading lessons of the spelling-book. It is more particularly designed as an immediate successor, in this respect, to the "Confederate Spelling Book," which has been so extensively adopted in the schools of the Confederate States.

The pieces have been selected with a view to interest and instruct the pupils, and at the same time to elevate their ideas, form correct tastes, and instil proper sentiments. Whatever seems most desirable for these purposes, among the literary materials that have become public property, has been freely appropriated ; suitable articles neither being rejected because familiar to adults, nor novelty sought for its own sake. At the same time, the selections have, by no means, been confined to the hackneyed list. It is believed that the exercises thus chosen, are well adapted to the capacity of those for whom they are designed, and will afford them much more real pleasure, as well as improvement, than the frivolous sentences which some suppose to be the best entertainment for juveniles.

TO TEACHERS.

This book is not designed to supersede the spelling-book, or suspend its use. Its leading purpose is to furnish suitable *reading* lessons for young pupils. It is not believed to be expedient to divide the learner's attention with other exercises, which are better pursued separately and in other books. "One thing at a time" is sound wisdom in study as in other employments.

The first thing to be carefully insisted on, in the young reader, is a clear, distinct articulation. This is indispensable to good reading. The habit of indistinct pronunciation is usually contracted in the early lessons of the pupil, and is ever afterwards difficult to overcome. It results from ignorance of words, or from a drawling, indolent tone, or from a haste which mutilates the words or runs them into each other.

A monotonous style of reading is another error into which the young reader is very liable to fall, unless closely watched. To avoid this, the lesson must be so carefully prepared that each word can be readily called at sight. There can be no good reading, and no improvement, where the learner must spell his way. Besides being familiar with the words of the lesson, the pupil must also understand its import, and catch its spirit. These will go far to ensure an easy utterance and natural tone, and the proper inflection and emphasis.

It should be borne in mind that a school-reader is not a mere story-book, to be hurried through, as such, and then flung aside for another. But the lessons are to be re-read and dwelt upon until familiarity and practice, aided by the instructions of the teacher, shall enable the young learner to give them a correct rendering.

It is recommended that the lesson be of such length as will permit each pupil to read the whole of it, or at least a large part of it, when the class is called to recite. This repetition will create a wholesome emulation among the pupils, and cause all to profit by the instructions given to each. The teacher should begin the recitation by reading the lesson to the pupils, calling their attention to particular points when necessary.

CONTENTS.

PIECES IN PROSE.

PIECES IN POETRY.

CONFEDERATE FIRST READER.

The Bad and Good Readers.

King Frederick was one day sitting in his palace, when a petition was placed in his hands. The King's eyes being dim, he called upon one of his pages to read it to him.

The boy was the son of a nobleman, but he was a poor reader. He pronounced his words badly, and hurried rapidly over them, in a dismal, sing-song tone. "Stop," said the King; "I cannot understand what you are reading. Send me some one else."

Another page now came forward; but he coughed, and hemmed, and cleared his throat, and uttered his words with a great swelling sound, and drawled them out so slowly, that the King took the paper from him, and told him to go out of the room.

A little girl, whom the King saw helping her father to weed the flower-beds, was next called for, to see if she could read the petition. She first glanced her eyes over it, and then read it aloud.

It was from a poor widow, whose husband had been killed in battle, and whose only son was now sent for, to serve in the army. As the son's health was very delicate, she begged the King to let him stay at home, and follow his business as a portrait-painter.

The little girl read the petition with such distinct pronunciation, and such natural tones, and with so much grace and feeling, that tears were standing in the King's eyes when she concluded. "Oh, now I know what it is about!" said he;

2

"but I never would have known, if the young men had read it to me."

The King then sent the little girl to tell the mother that her request was granted. He also employed the young man to paint his own portrait. The King likewise made the little girl's father, his chief-gardener; and as for her, he caused her to be well educated at his own expense. The two pages he dismissed from his service for a year, and told them to employ the time in learning to read.

Let all the children who may read the lessons in this book, study them well, and try to read like the little girl, and not like the two pages.

———

The Little Fish.—A Fable.

"Dear mother," said a little fish,
  "Pray, is not that a fly?
I'm very hungry, and I wish,
  You'd let me go and try."
"Sweet innocent," the mother cried,
  And started from her nook,
"That seeming fly is made to hide
  The sharpness of the hook."

Now, I have heard this little trout
  Was young and foolish too;
And so he thought he'd venture out,
  To see if it were true.
And round about the bait he played,
  With many a longing look;
And, "dear me," to himself he said,
  "I'm sure that's not a hook."

"I can but give one little bite,"
  Said he, "and so I will."
So on he went, when lo! it quite
  Stuck through his little gill.
And as he faint, and fainter, grew,
  With hollow voice he cried,
"Dear mother, had I minded you,
  I should not now have died."

The Honest Indian.

An Indian once met one of his white friends, who lived in a village not far from the Indian's wigwam, and asked him for a little tobacco to smoke in his pipe. The white man took a handful of loose tobacco out of his pocket, and gave it to him.

The next day the Indian came to the village, and enquired for the gentleman who had given him the tobacco. He said he had found a piece of money in the tobacco, and he wished to restore it to the owner.

The person to whom he addressed himself, told him the money was his, for it had been given to him; and that he ought to keep it, and not say any thing about it. But this advice did not please the honest Indian.

He pointed to his breast and said : " I got a good man, and a bad man in here. The good man say, ' This money is not yours ; you must return it to the owner.' The bad man say, ' It *is* yours ; for he gave it to you.' The good man say, ' That is not right; he gave you the tobacco, but not the money.' The bad man say, ' Never mind, you got it ; go buy some dram.' The good man say, ' No, no, you must not do so.' "

" So I don't know what to do, and I try to go to sleep; but the good man and the bad man kept talking all night, and trouble me ; and now I bring the money back I feel good."

God Sees Me.

God can see me every day ;
When I work and when I play,
When I read and when I talk,
When I run and when I walk,
When I eat and when I drink,
When I sit and when I think,
When I laugh and when I cry,
God is ever watching nigh.

When I'm quiet, when I'm rude,
When I'm naughty, when I'm good,
When I'm happy, when I'm sad,
When I'm sorry, when I'm glad,

When I pluck the scented rose,
That in the pretty garden grows,
When I crush the little fly,
God is watching from the sky.

When the sun gives heat and light,
When the stars are twinkling bright,
When the moon shines on my bed,
God still watches o'er my head.
Night or day, at church or fair,
God is ever, ever near,
Marking all I do or say,
Ready for the judgment day.

The Young Mouse.—A Fable.

A young mouse once lived in a house-keeper's pantry, and had a nice time there. Every day she dined on biscuit, or cold ham, or sugar; and often she got a taste of the sweetmeats. Sometimes she would peep into the dining-room; but when the cat was there, she would hasten back to her hole, dreadfully frightened.

One day, the young mouse came running to her mother in great joy. "Mother," said she, "the good people of the family have built me a house to live in, and they have placed it in the pantry. I am sure it is for me, for it is just big enough. The bottom is of wood, and it is covered all over with wires. I suppose they put the wires there to screen me from that ugly cat.

"And, mother, there is a little door, just big enough for me to go in. And they have put some nice cheese inside, just for me; and it smells so nice, that I could scarcely keep from going in, and taking possession. But, mother, I thought I would run and tell you, so that we might go in together, and stay there to-night; for it is big enough to hold us both."

"My dear child," said the mouse, "it is happy for you that you did not enter. This house, as you call it, is a trap, put there to catch you; and if you had entered it, you would never have come out again, except to be fed to the cat, or killed in some other way. Let this teach you never to trust to appearances, and always to ask the advice of older persons."

The Robin.

Away, pretty robin, fly home to your nest;
To make you my captive, I still should like best,
　And feed you with worms and with bread.
Your eyes are so sparkling, your feathers so soft,
Your little wings flutter so pretty aloft,
　And your breast is all colored with red.

But then 'twould be cruel to keep you, I know;
So stretch out your wings, little robin, and go;
　Fly home to your young ones again.
Go listen again to the notes of your mate,
And enjoy the green shade in your lonely retreat,
　Secure from the wind and the rain.

But when the leaves fall, and the winter winds blow,
And the green fields are covered all over with snow,
　And the clouds in white feathers descend;
When the springs are all ice, and the rivulets freeze,
And the long, shining icicles drop from the trees,
　Then, robin, remember your friend!

When with cold and with hunger, quite perished and weak,
Come tap at my window again with your beak,
　And gladly I'll let you come in.
You shall fly to my bosom or perch on my thumbs,
Or hop round the table and pick up the crumbs,
　And never be hungry again.

The Eagle and the Crow.—A Fable.

A hungry eagle gazed down upon a flock of sheep, and selecting a nice lamb, swooped upon him, and bore him away, bleating, to the forest, before the shepherd could do any thing to prevent it.

A crow that was sitting in a tree, near by, saw what had passed, and was filled with admiration at the action of the eagle. He resolved that he would be a grand bird, too, and pounce down upon the flock, as the eagle had done.

The crow accordingly selected the old bell-wether of the

flock, and darted upon him, fastened his claws in his wool, and attempted to fly away with him. He might as well have tried to fly away with the State House.

The shepherd was much amused at the silly crow, for he knew he could do no harm. He now went and caught him as he was entangled in the wool of the sheep; and he clipped his wings, and gave him to his children for their amusement.

This fable teaches us not to attempt what is beyond our capacity.

The Sparrow and the Hare.—A Fable.

A hare, on being seized by an eagle, raised the most piteous cries; for he knew that the eagle would soon tear him to pieces, and devour him.

A sparrow that was sitting upon a tree close by, and saw what had happened, began to make sport of the poor hare, and to laugh at his distress. "Why," said she, "do you sit there and be killed, my fine fellow? Up and away, I tell you! I am sure if you would try, so swift a creature as you are, could easily escape from an eagle."

As the sparrow was proceeding with this cruel raillery, there came a hawk and pounced down upon her, and commenced immediately to pick her feathers off, so that he might eat her.

The sparrow, too, now began to cry for mercy; but the hawk paid no attention to her; and the hare, which was just expiring, called to the sparrow and said, "Just now, you insulted me in my misfortune, and thought yourself very secure. Please show us how well you can bear the like, now that calamity has overtaken you also."

This fable teaches us to sympathize with the unfortunate, and never to make sport of their distresses.

The Squirrel.

The squirrel is happy, the squirrel is gay,
  Little Henry exclaimed to his brother.
He has nothing to do, or to think of, but play,
  And to jump from one bough to another.

But William was older and wiser, and knew
That all play, and no work, would not answer;
So he asked what the squirrel, in winter, would do,
If he spent all the summer a dancer.

The squirrel, dear Henry, is merry and wise,
For true wisdom and mirth go together.
He lays up, in summer, his winter supplies,
And then he don't mind the cold weather.

Creation of the World.

In the beginning, God created the heaven and the earth.

And the earth was without form, and void; and darkness was upon the face of the deep : and the spirit of God moved upon the face of the waters.

And God said, Let there be light: and there was light.

And God saw the light that it was good : and God divided the light from the darkness.

And God called the light day, and the darkness he called night.

And God made two great lights; the greater light to rule the day, and the lesser light to rule the night.   He made the stars also.

And God created great whales, and every living creature that moveth, which the waters brought forth abundantly after their kind, and every winged fowl after his kind.

And God made the beasts of the earth after his kind, and cattle after their kind, and every thing that creepeth upon the earth, after his kind.

And the Lord God formed man out of the dust of the ground, and breathed into his nostrils the breath of life; and man became a living soul.

And the Lord God planted a garden eastward in Eden ; and there he put the man whom he had formed.

And out of the ground, made the Lord God to grow every tree that is pleasant to the sight, and good for food; the tree of life also in the midst of the garden, and the tree of knowl-edge of good and evil,

And out of the ground, the Lord God formed every beast of the field, and every fowl of the air.

And Adam gave names to all cattle, and to the fowl of the air, and to every beast of the field.

And the Lord God caused a deep sleep to fall upon Adam, and he slept; and he took one of his ribs, and closed up the flesh instead thereof.

And the rib, which the Lord God had taken from man, made he a woman, and brought her unto the man.

And Adam said, This is now bone of my bones, and flesh of my flesh. She shall be called woman, because she was taken out of man.

On Behavior.

Do not stare at any one; for to do so, is a mark of rudeness and impudence.

Do not be forward to speak, when strangers or older persons are present.

Do not interrupt a person while he is speaking; but listen with attention and politeness, until he has finished.

Never whisper in company while others are conversing; for it is very rude and impolite to do so.

Be always respectful and obedient, to your parents and teachers, and to all who have the care of you.

Be affectionate to your friends, and kind and obliging to every body.

Never lose your temper with your playmates, or use rough words to them.

Do not rudely contradict any one, or use such angry expressions as I *will*, or I *won't*, or you *shan't*.

Always be very respectful to aged people, and to ladies; and render them attentions whenever there is opportunity.

Do not make sport of the lame, or the afflicted; but rather feel sorry for them, and show them kindness.

Do not be harsh, without cause, to servants, or those over whom you have authority. It is wrong to impose upon the helpless.

Remember that to be a gentleman, a person must have a kind heart, and be of gentle behavior, and polite manners.

The Bible.

Holy Bible, book divine,
Precious treasure, thou art mine !
Mine to tell me whence I came,
Mine to teach me what I am ;

Mine to chide me when I rove,
Mine to show a Saviour's love;
Mine art thou to guide my youth,
In the paths of love and truth ;

Mine to comfort in distress,
If the Holy Spirit bless ;
Mine to show by living faith,
Man can triumph over death.

Cruelty Punished.

A chimney-sweep was sitting on the steps of a house in London, eating a loaf of bread, which somebody had given him. A little dog stood near him, looking very wishfully at the bread, and begging for a piece, by all the signs which nature has taught dogs to make.

The boy took a delight in teasing the dog. He would hold out a piece of bread to him, and just as the animal was about to take hold of it, he would jerk it back.

At last the dog was too quick for the boy, and seized the bread before he could withdraw it. The cruel boy, thereupon, gave the dog a kick under the mouth, that sent him away yelping with pain.

A gentleman on the other side of the street had witnessed the conduct of the boy, and thought he would give him a les-son that would make him reflect upon his cruelty, and teach him to do better in future. So he held out a piece of money, and beckoned to the boy to come over and get it.

The boy ran across the street, and eagerly held out his hand to take hold of the money. But the gentleman, instead of letting him take it, gave him a severe rap over the knuckles with his cane, which made him roar with pain.

2*

"What did you do that for?" cried the boy. "Did you not offer me the money?"

"What did you hurt the dog for?" replied the gentleman. "Did you not offer him the bread? I have done this to show you how badly you treated the poor dog, and to put you in mind, never to act in such a manner again. For you must remember that dumb animals can feel as well as boys."

Uses of Arithmetic.

John wants to know, what three times three,
Added to five times two, may be.
Long has he puzzled o'er the sum,
Nor finds to what amount they come:
Yet he is old enough to know
Much more, and I must tell him so.
Let us ask Charles, for he can count,
And soon will tell us the amount.

Well, three times three are nine, he says;
And five times two, are ten, always.
When ten and nine are thus combined,
Nineteen's the number we shall find.
We ought to add up quick and well,
That what we spend, our books may tell,
And make us saving, to this end,
That we may give, as well as spend.

Anecdotes of Parrots.

Parrots may be taught to utter a great many words and sentences; and they often use them so appropriately, that they almost seem to be gifted with reason.

A gentleman once had a parrot that, every morning, would say to the servant, "Sally, Poll wants her breakfast;" and in the evening would say, "Sally, Poll wants her tea;" without ever making a mistake. Whenever she saw her master coming, she would say, "How do you do, Mr. Anderson?"

This parrot would whistle up the dogs, and drop bread out

of her cage to them; but when the dogs rushed up to get it, she would scream at them, "Get out, dogs.!" and make them run away. She would then laugh at them, and seem to be highly delighted at the trick she had played them.

There is a story told of a parrot that belonged to a king. One day a hawk caught her, and was bearing her away, when the parrot cried out, "Poll is a-riding!" This frightened the hawk, and he dropped the parrot. Unfortunately they were just over a river, so that the parrot fell into the water and was in danger of drowning.

As soon as the parrot found herself in the river, she cried out, "Twenty pounds for a boat!" A boatman, who was near by, rescued her. and, carrying her to the king, demanded the promised reward. The king told him he asked too much; but as the boatman insisted that the parrot had offered it, the king said he would leave it to the parrot to say how much he should pay him. As soon as he had said this, the parrot spoke up and said, "Give the knave a groat!"

Similes.

As proud as a peacock—as round as a pea;
As blithe as a lark—as brisk as a bee.
As light as a feather—as sure as a gun ;
As green as the grass—as brown as a bun.

As rich as a Jew—as warm as a toast ;
As cross as two sticks—as deaf as a post.
As sharp as a needle—as strong as an ox ;
As grave as a judge—as sly as a fox.

As old as the hills—as straight as a dart ;
As still as the grave—as swift as a hart.
As solid as marble—as firm as a rock ;
As soft as a plum—as dull as a block.

As pale as a lily—as blind as a bat ;
As white as a sheet—as black as my hat.
As yellow as gold—as red as a cherry ;
As wet as water—as brown as a berry.

As plain as a pikestaff—as big as a house ;
As flat as a table—as sleek as a mouse.
As tall as a steeple—as round as a cheese ;
As broad as 'tis long—as long as you please.

Learn to Swim.

Every body should learn to swim. It is not only a delightful exercise, but, by being able to swim, a person may sometimes save his own life, or that of another.

An amusing story is told of a man, who had become so
learned that he was called a philosopher ; but who had not
paid proper attention to other things. He was crossing a
river in a ferry-boat, at a place where the passage was not
safe ; but he was thinking only of his books, and of the pleasure which they gave him.

On the way across the river, the philosopher asked the
ferryman, if he understood arithmetic. The man answered,
that he had never heard of such a thing before. The philosopher told him he was very sorry, for he had lost a quarter
of his life by his ignorance.

The philosopher then asked him, if he had learned mathematics. The boatman smiled, and said he knew nothing
about it. The philosopher told him another quarter of his
life had been lost.

The philosopher then put a third question to the boatman,
and asked him if he understood astronomy. The boatman
told him no ; that he had never head of it before. The philosopher replied, that another quarter of his life had been lost.

Just at this moment the boat ran on a snag, and began to
sink. The ferryman threw off his coat, and got ready to save
himself by swimming. He then turned to the philosopher,
and asked him if he had learned to swim. The philosopher
told him he knew nothing about it. "Then," said the boatman, " the *whole* of your life is lost, for the boat is going to
the bottom."

And so, indeed, the philosopher's life would have been lost,
if the boatman had not saved him ; and the philosopher saw
that a knowledge of swimming was of more value at that
time, than all his arithmetic, and mathematics, and astronomy.

We must remember from this, that while we shoul.
all we can, and become as wise as possible, we must not ne.
common things.

Trust in Providence.

My times of sorrow, and of joy,
   Great God, are in thy hand !
My choicest comforts come from Thee,
   And go at thy command.

Though thou shouldst take them all away,
   Yet would I not repine.
Before they were possessed by me,
   They were entirely thine.

The world, with all its glittering stores,
   Is but a bitter sweet ;
When I attempt to pluck a rose,
   A prickling thorn I meet.

No perfect bliss can here be found ;
   The honey is mixed with gall.
'Midst changing scenes, and dying friends,
   Be Thou, my all in all !

The Eagle and the Cat.—A Fable.

One day, an eagle, that was flying along, high in the air,
saw what he supposed to be a fine, plump hare, sleeping on a
bank in the sunshine.

"Aha ! my fine fellow," said the eagle, " you are the very
thing I am looking for. I will spoil your nap for you very
quickly, and you shall make me a nice dinner."

So he immediately pounced down, swift as an arrow, on the
sleeping animal, stuck his sharp claws in his back, and rose
again in the air, and started to fly away with him to a hill
top, where he intended to eat him.

But it was a very little time before the eagle found out

that he had made a great mistake. Instead of a hare, that could do nothing but cry for mercy, he had caught a cat, with sharp teeth, and with claws as keen as his own.

The cat was very much surprised, when it first woke up, to find itself pinched so in the back, and flying through the air and over the tree tops, so very rapidly. But it soon found out what was the matter, and so it laid hold of the eagle with might and main.

The eagle was now the one to be surprised; and he begged the cat's pardon, and said if the cat would let him go, he would let the cat go. But the cat would not agree to that; for he was not willing to fall from a such a height. So he made the eagle fly back, and put him down safely on the same bank where he had found him; and the eagle was glad enough to get rid of the cat on these terms.

Sometimes, persons who attempt to injure others, find themselves as much mistaken as the eagle was, when he flew upon the cat.

The Way to be Happy.

How pleasant it is, at the end of the day,
   No follies to have to repent;
But reflect on the past, and be able to say,
   That my time has been properly spent.

When I've done all my business with patience and care,
   And been good, and obliging, and kind,
I lie on my pillow, and sleep away there,
   With a happy and peaceable mind.

But instead of all this, if it must be confessed,
   That I, careless and idle, have been;
I lie down as usual, and go to my rest,
   But feel discontented within.

Then, as I don't like all the trouble I've had,
   In future, I'll try to prevent it;
For I never am naughty without being sad,
   Or good without being contented.

The Birth of Jesus.

And there were in the same country, shepherds abiding in the field, keeping watch over their flock by night.

And, lo, the angel of the Lord came upon them, and the glory of the Lord shone round about them; and they were sore afraid.

And the angel said unto them, Fear not: for, behold, I bring you good tidings of great joy, which shall be to all people.

For unto you is born this day, in the city of David, a Saviour, which is Christ the Lord.

And this shall be a sign unto you? Ye shall find the babe wrapped in swaddling clothes, lying in a manger.

And suddenly there was with the angel, a multitude of the heavenly host, praising God, and saying,

Glory to God in the highest, and on earth peace, good will towards men.

And it came to pass, as the angels were gone away from them into heaven, the shepherds said one to another, Let us now go even unto Bethlehem, and see this thing which is come to pass, which the Lord hath made known unto us.

And they came with haste, and found Mary and Joseph, and the babe lying in a manger.

And when they had seen it, they made known abroad the saying which was told them concerning this child.

Filial Love .Rewarded.

Frederick the Great, King of Prussia, rung his bell one day, but nobody answered. He looked into the room where the youth whom he had for a page, was usually in waiting, and found him fast asleep on a sofa.

The King was going to awake him, when he perceived the end of a letter projecting from his pocket. Being curious to know its contents, he took the letter and read it. It was a letter from his mother, thanking him for sending her so large a part of his wages, to assist her in her distress; and it concluded by praying God to bless him, for his filial attention to her wants.

The King was much pleased with the letter, and was glad

to find that his page was so affectionate and dutiful a son. He returned softly to his room and got a purse of money, and then came back, and slipped both the purse and the letter, into the page's pocket. He then returned to his own room again, and rung the bell so violently that the page awoke, and came to him.

"You have slept well!" said the King. The page was very much confused, and made an apology; but, in his embarrassment, he happened to put his hand into his pocket, and thus discovered the purse of money. He drew it out, turned pale, and, looking at the King, he burst into tears, without being able to speak a word.

"What is the matter?" asked the King. "What ails you?" "Ah sire," said the youth, throwing himself at his feet, "somebody wishes to ruin me! I do not know how this money came into my pocket."

The King kindly told him to give himself no uneasiness, but to send the money to his mother. He also said, "Tell her I am glad she has so dutiful a son; and assure her, in my name, that I will take care both of her and you."

Early Piety.

Happy the child, whose tender years,
　Receive instruction well;
Who hates the sinner's path and fears,
　The road that leads to hell.

When we devote our youth to God,
　'Tis pleasing in His eyes;
A flower, when offered in the bud,
　Is no vain sacrifice.

'Tis easier work, if we begin
　To fear the Lord betimes;
While sinners, that grow old in sin,
　Are hardened in their crimes.

'Twill save us from a thousand snares,
　To mind religion young;
Grace will improve our following years,
　And make our virtue strong.

To Thee, Almighty God, to Thee,
　Our childhood we resign !
'Twill please us to look back and see,
　That our whole lives were thine !

Let the sweet work of prayer and praise,
　Employ my youthful breath ;
Thus I'm prepared for length of days,
　Or fit for early death.

Musical Mice.

Mice are sometimes very fond of music, and it has a wonderful effect upon them. It takes away all their fear of people, and sometimes makes them play very curious antics.

A gentleman of Norfolk City, in Virginia, was once sitting alone in his chamber, playing his flute. In a few minutes, he saw a little mouse creep out of his hole, and advance towards the chair in which he was sitting. Whenever the gentleman stopped playing, the mouse would run into his hole ; but it would come back, when he heard the flute again.

The actions of the mouse, while listening to the music, were very amusing. It would shut its eyes, crouch on the floor, and seem to be in an ecstasy of delight. At last it went away, and the gentleman never saw it again.

There was once a mouse of this sort, on board an English ship. One of the officers was playing a plaintive air on the violin, when the mouse ran out into the middle of the floor, and began to cut the most violent capers. It leaped about as if it were frantic with joy ; and it became more and more violent every moment, until it finally fell down, and died from the excitement.

A gentleman, of Virginia, was one day amusing himself by playing some airs upon the piano, when a little mouse came out to listen. It was so much pleased, that it approached nearer ; and finally it climbed up on the gentleman's shoulder, and then out on his arm, where it sat still, and allowed him to take it in his hand, and put it in his pocket.

There are many other animals that are much affected by music. Snakes have been charmed by it ; and a negro man once kept a pack of wolves from eating him up, by playing the fiddle to them.

Employment.

Who'll come and play with me under the tree?
My sisters have left me alone;
My sweet little sparrow, come hither to me,
And play with me while they are gone.

O no, little Anna, I can't come indeed,
I've no time to idle away.
I've got all my dear little children to feed,
And my nest to new cover with hay.

Pretty bee, do not buzz about over the flower,
But come here and play with me now;
The sparrow won't come and stay with me an hour,
But say, pretty bee—wilt not thou?

O no, little Anna, for dost thou not see,
Those must work who would prosper and thrive?
If I play, they will call me a sad idle bee,
And perhaps turn me out of the hive.

Stop! stop! little ant, do not run off so fast,
Wait with me a little, and play:
I hope I shall find a companion at last;
Thou art not so busy as they.

O no, little Anna, I can't stay with thee;
We're not made to play, but to labor.
There is always something or other for me
To do for myself, or a neighbor.

What, then, have they all some employment but me,
Who lay lounging here like a dunce?
O then, like the ant, and the sparrow, and bee,
I'll go to my lesson at once.

Monkeys and their Tricks.

Monkeys are very cunning and mischievous little animals,
that are found in warm countries. They have a face some-

ing like a man's, and they can use their fore-feet for hands.
they have long tails, with which they swing to trees, and
ey are remarkably active.

Monkeys are great rogues. The wild monkeys frequently
under the gardens of persons, who live near the forests
iich they infest. When they go on these stealing expedi-
ous, they place some of their number to act as sentinels, so
at it is very hard to creep upon them.

Monkeys are very easily tamed, and afford a great deal of
nusement by their cunning tricks; but they have to be
atched very closely, for they are always in some mischief.
hey will catch the cat and use her claws to pull chestnuts
ut of the fire. They will snatch things out of the pot if the
ook turns her back, and they are constantly trying to imitate
very thing they see others do.

There was once on board a ship, an African monkey named
ack, that gave great amusement to the passengers and sailors.
The first thing he would do in the morning, was to upset the
parrot's cage, and make the lump of sugar roll out, when he
would instantly catch it up and eat it.

He would snatch the caps off the sailors' heads, and if they
were not very quick, would throw them overboard. When
the cook was preparing breakfast, he would sit near the grate,
and watch his chance to steal something. He sometimes
burnt his fingers by these rogueries, but it did not cure him
of them.

The captain would sometimes turn the ship's pigs on deck,
that they might run about for exercise. This was always a
grand time for Jack. He would spring upon the pigs' backs,
and ride them all over the ship. The pigs would be very
much frightened, and run with all their might. Sometimes
they would upset Jack, and then the sailors would laugh at
him, which he did not like.

There was a little black monkey on board the same ship.
Jack caught him one day, and painted him. He held him
by the back of the neck with one hand, and with the other,
he took the painter's brush, and covered him all over with
white paint. Jack was so afraid that the captain would whip
him for this, that he scampered up to the maintop, and staid
there three days before he would come down. A lady, however, who was on board, persuaded the captain to pardon
him; and so Jack escaped the punishment which he knew he
deserved.

The Lion and the Mouse.—A Fable.

A lion lay sleeping in the forest one day, when some m[...] began to amuse themselves by running over him. He su[...] denly roused, and catching at a mouse that did not get aw[...] as quickly as the others, he seized him in his paw, and w[...] about to kill him.

The poor mouse was terribly alarmed, and begged hard f[...] his life. The lion looked at the little trembler, and like[...] noble animal, thought it would be a discreditable thing fo[...] one so big as he, to hurt one so small as the mouse. So h[...] generously forgave the mouse for his mischief, and told hi[...] to go free. The mouse lost no time, but scampered away a[...] fast as he could.

It happened a few days afterwards, that the lion was hunt[...] ing in the same woods. While he was not watching his step[...] very closely, he got entangled in a net, which a cunnin[...] hunter had set for him. He was now as much frightened a[...] the little mouse had been, and he roared with terror.

The mouse heard him, and knew by his voice, that it wa[...] the same lion which had given him his life. He immediate[...] hurried to the lion's assistance, as fast as his little legs cou[...] carry him. When he saw what was the matter, he told th[...] lion not to be uneasy, for he would soon set him free.

So the mouse went to work with his sharp little teeth, and soon gnawed the cords in two, in so many places, that the lion got out without any difficulty. The lion was very much surprised and pleased, when he found that the helpless little mouse had been able to render him such great service.

This fable teaches us to be kind to the weak and helpless; and to remember that there is no person so much below us, that he may not be able to render a good service in time of need.

To the Lady-Bird.

Lady-Bird, Lady-Bird, fly away home!
The field-mouse has gone to her nest;
The daisies have shut up their sleepy red eyes,
And the bees and the birds are at rest.

Lady-Bird, Lady-Bird, fly away home!
The glowworm is lighting her lamp;
The dew is falling fast, and your fine speckled wings
Will flag with the cumbering damp.

Lady-Bird, Lady-Bird, fly away home!
Good luck if you reach it at last;
The owl is abroad, and the bat's on the roam,
Sharp set from their tedious fast.

Lady-Bird, Lady-Bird, fly away home!
And if not gobbled up on the way,
You should reach your snug nest in the old willow-tree,
You are lucky,—and I have no more to say.

The Faithful Dog.

A gentleman, accompanied by his dog, was travelling in the West of England, when night overtook him. Not being acquainted with the road, he soon lost his way, and fell into a coal-pit thirty feet deep.

All night, the dog ran round and round the mouth of the pit, barking and howling, as if he was trying to call somebody there to extricate his master. But nobody came.

The next morning, he went back to the house where his master had last staid. When he got there, he did every thing he could, to attract the attention of the servants. He would look at them and whine, and would throw himself on his back before them, as if he was begging them to do something.

The servants offered him food, but he would not eat it. He did nothing but howl, and run backwards and forwards about the door, and give other signs of being in great distress about something. But the servants could not understand him.

At last, the lady of the house, thinking that something must be the matter, told one of the servants to follow him wherever he might go. The dog was now delighted, and rapidly led the way to the pit into which his master had fallen. The gentleman had given himself up for lost, and expected nothing but to starve to death; but the servant went back for help, and soon returned and rescued him from his terrible situation.

Old Cato.

Do you think our poor dog, to the stable we'll send,
  Because he's grown feeble and old ?
No, no, every night, quite secure from alarm,
Old Cato must sleep in the kitchen so warm ;
  He shan't be turn'd out in the cold.

I remember the time when so frisky and gay,
  He would bark at each one that he met;
And watch round the house while asleep we all lay,
If a base lurking robber came prowling that way: '
  These things I can never forget.

And when Tom, the shepherd, would drive out the sheep,
  He'd watch by the side of the fold ;
No, no, my poor Cato, secure from all harm,
Shall eat and shall drink in the kitchen so warm ;
  He shan't be turn'd out in the cold.

The Indian and His Dog.

A family by the name of Lefevre, lived near the Blu
Ridge mountains, many years ago. An Indian, named Tewe
nissa, frequently called to spend the night, when his journe}
ings led him past the house of Lefevre. He was alway
cordially welcomed, and kindly entertained.

One day, when Tewenissa, laden with furs, stopped at th
house of his friend, he found no one at home, but an old ne
gro woman. "Where is my brother?" asked the India1
"Ah sir," said the woman, "his little boy Derick, only fou
years old, the same that you loved to take upon your kne￼
wandered away into the forest on yesterday, and is lost; an
all the neighbors are helping the distressed parents to loo
for him."

Tewenissa was grieved when he learned of the sorrow ￼
his friend's family, and the misfortune to his little favorite
He sounded the horn, and called in the hunting party; an
then he told Mr. Lefevre that he would find his little boy.

Tewenissa then asked for the shoes and stockings that littl

Derick had last worn. He next called his faithful dog Oniah, and made him smell them. Taking the house for a centre, he then commenced drawing a circle all around it with his stick, making Oniah smell the earth as he went.

The circle was not completed before the sagacious dog began to bark. He had discovered the scent, and he commenced to follow the little boy's track, barking as he went. The Indian followed as fast as he could, and so did little Derick's parents, and the rest of the party; but the dog ran so fast that he was soon out of sight.

Half an hour afterwards, they heard Oniah bark again, and soon they saw him returning. He was frisky with joy; so that the Indian knew at once, that he had found the little boy, but whether he was dead or alive could not yet be known. The dog now led the way with Tewenissa following close at his heels, until they came to little Derick lying at the foot of a large tree.

The little boy was alive, but extremely weak and exhausted, so that he could not have lived much longer. Tewenissa took him up in his arms, and carried him to his parents, who were almost overcome with joy. By proper treatment, little Derick was soon as well as ever.

The gratitude of the parents, to the Indian and to his dog, was so great that for a long time they could do nothing but weep; and Tewenissa was almost as much pleased as they were. And the neighbors, when they separated, went to their homes highly delighted with the good Indian, and his wonderful dog.

Kind Words.

A little word in kindness spoken,
    A motion or a tear,
Has often healed the heart that's broken,
    And made a friend sincere.

A word, a look, has crushed to earth,
    Full many a budding flower,
Which, had a smile but owned its birth,
    Would bless life's darkest hour.

Then deem it not an idle thing,
A pleasant word to speak;
The face you wear, the thoughts you bring,
A heart may heal or break.

The Good-Natured Dog.

Some dogs are very fond of playing with little boys, and will take as much pleasure in the game, as any of them. They will run after a ball, and bring it back to the one who threw it, and do many other amusing things.

There was a large dog, named Bernard, that belonged to the teacher of a large school of boys in Virginia. Bernard seemed to know as well as any one, when the time approached for play; and when the boys came running out into the yard, he would meet them, ready to take his share in their amusements.

His favorite sport was to take a stick in his mouth and walk towards them, nodding his head at them, as if he was challenging them to catch him and take the stick away. A troop of boys would immediately pursue him, and the game would begin. Bernard would run just fast enough to keep them from catching him. The boys would sometimes surround him, and think they were sure of him; but just as they would grab at him, he would jump between two of them, or dart between their legs, and away he would go. Sometimes they would get near enough to catch at his bushy tail; but he would make a sudden leap and elude them again.

At last, after the chase had been kept up till they were all tired, Bernard would let them have the pleasure of catching him, and taking his stick away; and then they would jump on his back, or do any thing with him that they wished, and he would never hurt them or get angry. Indeed, the boys all considered him one of the best playmates they had.

The Lark and her Young Ones.—A Fable.

A lark having made her nest in a wheat-field, the wheat became ripe before the young larks were able to fly. Being afraid that the farmer would cut down his wheat before she had provided another place for her little ones, she directed them, while she was gone to get food for them, to listen to what they might hear the farmer say about beginning his harvest.

The old lark then went out; but when she came home again, the little birds ran to her and said, "Oh, mother, take us away from here just as soon as you can; for while you were gone we heard the farmer tell his sons that the wheat was ripe, and that they must go and ask some of his neighbors to come early to-morrow morning, and help him to cut it down."

"If that is what he said, you need not be afraid, my children," said the old lark. "If the farmer depends upon his neighbors to do his work for him, he will find himself mistaken, and we shall be very safe where we are. So lie down in your nest, and give yourselves no uneasiness."

The next day, when the old lark was going out, she gave her young ones the same directions. In the evening, when she returned, the little larks told her the neighbors had not come to cut down the wheat; but they begged her to move them immediately; for they said that the farmer had told his sons to go and request his friends and relations to come early the next morning, and assist him.

"We are in no danger yet, my children," said the old lark; "for as long as he looks to his friends and relations, to do for him what he ought to do for himself, his wheat will go unharvested. So we will make ourselves quiet, and stay in our nest, for we have no cause for anxiety at present."

The next day the mother-lark again told her young ones to listen to what the farmer might say, and tell her when she came back. In the evening, when she came home, the little larks told her that the farmer had been there with his sons, but that his friends and relations did not come to assist him. The farmer then told his sons to grind their scythes, and get ready, and that early to-morrow morning, they would begin and harvest the wheat themselves.

"We must now prepare to leave immediately," said the old lark; "for when a man resolves to do his work himself, and to depend upon nobody else, the work is pretty sure to be done; but as long as he depends on friends or neighbors, he is almost sure to effect nothing." So the old lark moved the little birds

3

that same evening, into another field; and sure enough, the next morning the farmer and his sons came, and cut down the wheat.

This fable teaches us to do our work ourselves, and not rely upon others to do it for us. If we trust to others, they will often disappoint us; and it will also produce habits of laziness and dependence, which will prevent us from ever being prosperous or useful.

The Ant Hill.

Take care, little Richard! don't hurry so fast
    Look well to your footsteps, my boy—
If on that ant hill you carelessly tread,
    You will many hours' labor destroy.

For these poor little ants have been working all day
    To build up that minikin pile;
One grain at a time they have lifted it out,
    And been patient as lambs all the while.

They have scoop'd out a little snug hole in the earth,
    Their winter's provisions to hold;
And to serve for a bedroom, when summer is past,
    Secure from the rain and the cold.

How cruel 'twould be to kick over a house
    Which has cost so much toil to prepare!
Step aside, little Richard, and learn to be wise,
    From the busy ant's provident care.

If with diligence now, you will study your book,
    And be careful each moment to save;
Should you live, my dear child, to the winter of age,
    What a fine stock of knowledge you'll have!

But let this one truth sink deep in your heart,
    And keep it forever in mind;
That your learning will be to no purpose, unless
    You are humble, and modest, and kind.

For learning alone will not make you belov'd,
    If you're cruel, or selfish, or vain;
But a sweet, lowly temper will win every heart,
    And the blessing of Heaven obtain.

The Ferocious Dog.

Some dogs are so vicious that it is not safe to let them run at large. They are kept chained in the day time, and only turned loose at night for the purpose of guarding their owners' houses and other property, from thieves and robbers. Sometimes they get loose during the day, and do much mischief.

A drayman's horse once escaped from him in a certain city, and commenced to gallop up the street. The drayman started after him, and called to the people whom he saw, to stop the horse, and help him to catch him again.

A number of persons ran out into the street to head the horse, and with them there went a bull-dog, which is one of the fiercest kinds of dogs. The bull-dog instantly sprang at the horse, and seized him by the upper lip.

This frightened the horse so much, and gave him so much pain, that he became frantic. So he ran along several streets with all his might, the bull-dog hanging to his lip all the time. At length a crowd got in front of the horse, and stopped him; but he was so wild with pain and fear, that he ran through a hardware store, and into a parlor where the family were at tea.

The family were not expecting such a visitor as that. They had not invited a horse to take supper with them, with a bull-dog hanging to his lip. But they had not much time to ask questions; for the horse upset their table, and broke their china, and spoiled their supper, before they knew what was the matter.

A number of men now seized the horse, and held him, while others tried to beat off the savage dog. But all their efforts were in vain; for the bull-dog hung on to the horse's lip, with merciless and unyielding grip. At last one of the company had to take a knife and cut the dog's throat, in order to relieve the horse. It might perhaps have been done by taking a stick, and prizing open the dog's mouth.

If ever you see a horse frantic with fright, you must be very watchful, or he may run over you; for horses in that state, will dash into a house or against a tree, or butt their brains out against a wall, without seeming to know or care what they are doing.

God Seen in All Things.

Thou art, O God! the life and light,
   Of all this wondrous world we see;
Its glow by day, its smile by night,
   Are but reflections caught from thee.
Where'er we turn, thy glories shine,
And all things fair and bright are thine.

When day, with farewell beam, delays,
   Among the golden clouds of even,
And we can almost think we gaze,
   Through opening vistas, into heaven:
Those hues, that make the sun's decline
So soft, so radiant, Lord! are thine.

When night, with wings of stormy gloom,
   O'ershadows all the earth and skies,
Like some dark beauteous bird, whose plume
   Is sparkling with unnumbered dyes;
That sacred gloom, those fires divine,
So grand, so countless, Lord! are thine.

When youthful Spring around us breathes,
   Thy spirit warms her fragrant sigh;
And every flower that Summer wreathes,
   Is born beneath thy kindling eye.
Where'er we turn, thy glories shine,
And all things fair and bright, are thine.

Show and Use—The Two Colts.

A nobleman once had a beautiful blooded colt, and also a mule-colt. He gave the young horse to his neighbor, Mr.

Scamper, while the little mule went to a very poor man, who made his living by cutting wood.

Mr. Scamper was greatly delighted with his fine colt; and indeed, as he grew up, he became still handsomer. His color was bright bay, with a white star in his forehead, and his hair was fine and smooth, and as glossy as silk.

Mr. Scamper was resolved to train him up for a race-horse; for he was too fine a horse to be put to any useful purpose. So he was kept in a warm stable, and fed with the best of corn and hay, and was duly curried and rubbed, and regularly exercised. Indeed, Mr. Scamper treated him with as much care and tenderness, as he did his own children.

When this fine horse was three years old, Mr. Scamper sent him away to be trained for the race-course. The expense of this, was greater than Mr. Scamper could afford; so he had to take his children from the good school to which they were going, and send them to an inferior one, because it was cheaper.

The next year the young racer was placed upon the turf. He was beaten the first race; but he came out second. In the next race, he was successful; and Mr. Scamper was almost crazy with joy. Mr. Scamper now gave his whole attention to racing; and at last he became so excited, that he made up a race in which he bet all he was worth on his horse. The race was lost, and Mr. Scamper was broken up and ruined.

The little mule, meanwhile, had grown up also, but through a great deal of hardship. He had to live on what he could find in the lanes and among the bushes; and in winter, he had no stable to shelter in. As soon as he was big enough to ride, two or three of the children would mount him at a time, and beat him along with sticks. But he grew up healthy and strong.

His owner then set him to hauling wood to market, and in this way the mule was very profitable to him. He soon made enough money, to buy a plenty of food for his mule, which thus became fat and greatly improved. After awhile, he was able, out of the earnings of his mule, to buy a horse and cow; and he soon became quite a farmer, and grew rich. So that while Mr. Scamper's present ruined him, because his horse was thought too fine for service, the mule made the wood-cutter's fortune, because he put him to a good use.

How to Tell Bad News.

Mr. H.—Ha! Steward, how are you, my old boy? How do things go on at home?

Steward.—Bad enough, your honor. The magpie's dead.

Mr. H.—Poor Mag! so he's gone. How came he to die?

Stew.—Over-ate himself, sir.

Mr. H.—Did he, indeed? a greedy villain! Why, what did he get that he liked so well?

Stew.—Horse-flesh, sir; he died of eating horse-flesh.

Mr. H.—How came he to get so much horse-flesh?

Stew.—All your father's horses, sir.

Mr. H.—What! are they dead, too?

Stew.—Ay, sir; they died of over-work.

Mr H.—And why were they over-worked, pray?

Stew.—To carry water, sir.

Mr. H.—To carry water! and what were they carrying water for?

Stew.—Sure, sir, to put out the fire.

Mr. H.—Fire! what fire?

Stew.—O, sir, your father's house is burned down to the ground.

Mr. H.—My father's house burned down! and how came it set on fire?

Stew.—I think, sir, it must have been the torches.

Mr. H.—Torches! what torches?

Stew.—At your mother's funeral.

Mr. H.—Alas! has my mother died?

Stew.—Ah, poor lady, she never looked up after it.

Mr. H.—After what?

Stew.—The loss of your father.

Mr. H.—My father gone, too?

Stew.—Yes, poor gentleman, he took to his bed as soon as he heard of it.

Mr. H.—Heard of what?

Stew.—The bad news, sir, and please your honor.

Mr H.—What! more miseries? more bad news? No! you can add nothing more!

Stew.—Yes, sir; your bank has failed, and your credit is lost, and you are not worth a shilling in the world. I made bold, sir, to come to wait on you about it, for I thought you would like to hear the news.

Contented John.

There was honest John Tompkins, a hedger and ditcher,
Although he was poor, he did not sigh to be richer;
For all such vain wishes, to him were prevented,
By a fortunate habit of being contented.

If cold was the weather, or dear was the food,
John never was found in a murmuring mood;
For this, he was constantly heard to declare,—
What he could not prevent, he could cheerfully bear.

For why should I grumble and murmur, he said;
If I cannot get meat, I can surely get bread;
And though fretting may make my calamities deeper,
It never can cause bread and cheese to be cheaper.

If John was afflicted with sickness or pain,
He wished himself better, but did not complain,
Nor lie down to fret, in despondence and sorrow,
But said—that he hoped he would be better to-morrow.

If any one wronged him, or treated him ill,
Why, John was good-natured and sociable still;
For he said, that revenging the injury done,
Would be making two bad men, where there need be but one.

And thus honest John, though his station was humble,
Passed through this sad world, without even a grumble;
And I wish that some folks, who are greater and richer,
Would copy John Tompkins, the hedger and ditcher.

The Earth and Its Inhabitants.

It was four thousand and four years before the coming of
Christ, or nearly six thousand years ago, when this earth was
first inhabited by men.

There are now five varieties or races of men found on the
earth. They are distinguished from each other partly by their
different colors. There are the White race, the Yellow race,
the Red race, the Brown race, and the Black race.

The White people live chiefly in Europe, and they came ace to America. The Yellow and the Brown people, live iefl, in Asia, and the great Islands near Asia. The Black ple jive in Africa, or came from there. The Red people, , .!ed Indians, live in America.

America was not known to White people, until nearly four hundred years ago A brave man, named Christopher Columbus, was the first to discover it. After sailing, for many months and days, across the dark waters of the ocean, where nobody had ventured before, he came in sight of America on the 11th October, in the year 1492.

When America was discovered, it was grown up in forests. There were no cities, or towns, or houses, such as we have now ; and no farms and meadows, and no ships and steamboats on the rivers. The woods were filled with all sorts of wild animals, and the Indians lived chiefly by hunting them with their bows and arrows.

When the White men first came here, the Indians thought that they and their ships, had dropped down from the sky. They supposed that they were superior beings, and were very much afraid of them, and treated them generally with great kindness.

It was not long, however, before the White people began to oppress them; and then there arose war and fighting, in which the Indians behaved very cruelly, but were always vanquished, and a great many of them were destroyed; so that there are very few Indians now, compared with the number that were here when Columbus discovered America.

Gratitude.

Whene'er I take my walks abroad,
  How many poor I see !
What shall I render to my God,
  For all his gifts to me ?

Not more than others I deserve,
  Yet God has given me more ;
For I have food while others starve,
  Or beg from door to door.

How many children, on the street,
   Half naked I behold;
While I am clothed from head to feet,
   And sheltered from the cold.

While some poor creatures scarce can tell,
   Where they may lay their head,
I have a home wherein to dwell,
   And rest upon my bed.

While others early learn to swear,
   And curse, and lie, and steal,
Lord! I am taught thy name to fear,
   And do thy holy will.

Are these thy favors, day by day,
   To me above the rest?
Then let me love thee more than they,
   And try to serve thee best!

Heaven.

The rose is sweet, but it is surrounded with thorns; the spring is pleasant, but it is soon past; the rainbow is glorious, but it vanisheth away; life is good, but it is quickly swallowed up in death.

There is a place of rest for the righteous; in that land there is light without any cloud, and flowers that never fade. Myriads of happy souls are there, singing praises to God.

That country is Heaven: it is the country of those that are good; and nothing that is wicked must inhabit there. This earth is pleasant, for it is God's earth, and it is filled with delightful things.

But that country is better: there we shall not grieve any more, nor be sick any more, nor do wrong any more. In that country there are no quarrels; all love one another with dear love.

When our friends die, and are laid in the cold ground, we see them here no more; but there we shall embrace them, and never be parted from them again. There we shall see all the good men which we read of.

There we shall see Jesus, who is gone before us to that happy ce ; there we shall behold the glory of the high God.

The Christian Race.

Awake, my soul! stretch every nerve,
  And press with vigor on !
A heavenly race demands thy zeal,
  And an immortal crown.

A cloud of witnesses around,
  Hold thee in full survey.
Forget the steps already trod,
  And onward urge thy way.

'Tis God's all-animating voice,
  That calls thee from on high,
'Tis his own hand presents the prize,
  To thine aspiring eye :

My soul! with sacred ardour fired,
  The glorious prize pursue ;
And meet with joy, the high command,
  To bid the earth adieu.

The Seasons.

Who is this beautiful maiden that approaches, clothed in a robe of green light? She has a garland of flowers on her head, and flowers spring up wherever she sets her foot. The snow which covered the fields, and the ice which was on the rivers, melt away when she breathes upon them.

The young lambs frisk about her, and the birds warble to welcome her coming. When they see her, they begin to choose their mates, and to build their nests. Youths and maidens, have ye seen this beautiful virgin? If ye have, tell me who she is, and what is her name.

Who is this that cometh from the south, thinly clad in a light, transparent garment? Her breath is hot and sultry. She seeks the clear streams, the crystal brooks, to bathe her languid limbs. The brooks and rivulets fly from her, and are dried up at her approach. She cools her parched lips with berries, and the grateful acids of fruits. The tanned hay-makers welcome her coming; and the sheep-shearer, who clips the fleeces off his flock with his sounding shears.

When she cometh, let me lie under the thick shade of a spreading beech-tree,—let me walk with her in the early morning, when the dew is yet upon the grass,—let me wander with her in the soft twilight, when the shepherd shuts his fold, and the star of the evening appears. Who is she that cometh from the south? Youth and maidens, tell me, if ye know, who she is, and what is her name.

Who is he that cometh with sober pace, stealing upon us unawares? His garments are red with the blood of the grape, and his temples are bound with a sheaf of ripe wheat. His hair is thin, and begins to fall, and the auburn is mixed with mourning gray. He shakes the brown nuts from the tree. He winds the horn, and calls the hunters to their sport. The gun sounds. The trembling partridge and the beautiful pheasant flutter bleeding in the air, and fall dead at the sportsman's feet. Youth and maidens, tell me, if ye know, who he is, and what is his name.

Who is he that cometh from the north, in furs and warm wool? He wraps his cloak close about him. His head is bald; his beard is made of sharp icicles. He loves the blazing fire high piled upon the hearth, and the wine sparkling in the glass. He binds skates to his feet, and skims over the frozen lakes. His breath is piercing and cold, and no little flower dares to peep above the surface of the ground when he is by. Whatever he touches, turns to ice. Youth and maidens, do you see him? He is coming upon us, and soon will be here. Tell me, if ye know, who he is, and what is his name.

The Creator Greater than His Works.

Come, and I will show you what is beautiful. It is a rose fully blown. See how she sits upon her mossy stem, like the queen of all the flowers! Her leaves glow like fire; the air is filled with her sweet odor; she is the delight of every eye.

She is beautiful, but there is a fairer than she. He that

made the rose, is more beautiful than the rose : He is all lovely:
He is the delight of every heart.

I will show you what is strong.   The lion is strong.   When
he raiseth himself from his lair, when he shaketh his mane,
when the voice of his roaring is heard, the cattle of the field
fly, and the wild beasts of the desert hide themselves, for he
is very terrible.

The lion is strong, but He that made the lion is stronger
than he.   His anger is terrible : He could make us die in a
moment, and no one could save us from His hand.

I will show you what is glorious.   The sun is glorious.
When he shineth in the clear sky, and is seen all over the
earth, he is the most glorious object the eye can behold.

The sun is glorious, but He that made the sun is more glorious than he.   The eye beholdeth Him not, for His brightness
is more dazzling than we could bear.   He seeth in all dark
places, by night as well as by day, and the light of His countenance is over all His works.

Who is this great name, and what is he called, that my lips
may praise him ?

This great name is God.   He made all things, but He is
himself more excellent than they.   They are beautiful, but He
is beauty ; they are strong, but He is strength ; they are perfect, but He is perfection.

The Old Horse.

No, children, he shall not be sold ;
   Go lead him home, and dry your tears.
'Tis true, he's blind, and lame, and old,
   But he has served us twenty years.

Well, has he served us,—gentle, strong,
   And willing, through life's varied stage ;
And having toiled for us so long,
   We will protect him in his age.

Our debt of gratitude to pay,
   His faithful merits to requite,
His play-ground be the field by day,
   A shed shall shelter him at night.

A life of labor was his lot;
    He always tried to do his best.
Poor fellow, now we'll grudge thee not,
    A little liberty and rest.

Go, then, old friend; thy future fate,
    To range the fields from harness free;
And just below the cottage gate,
    I'll go and build a shed for thee.

The Ten Commandments.

And God spake all these words, saying:

I. Thou shalt have no other gods before me.

II. Thou shalt not make unto thee any graven image, or the likeness of any thing that is in heaven above, or that is in the earth beneath, or that is in the waters under the earth:

Thou shalt not bow down thyself to them, nor serve them: for I the Lord thy God, am a jealous God, visiting the iniquity of the fathers upon the children, unto the third and fourth generations of them that hate me;

And showing mercy unto thousands of them that love me and keep my commandments.

III. Thou shalt not take the name of the Lord thy God in vain; for the Lord will not hold him guiltless that taketh his name in vain.

IV. Remember the Sabbath-day to keep it holy.

Six days shalt thou labor and do all thy work:

But the seventh is the Sabbath of the Lord thy God: in it thou shalt not do any work, thou nor thy son nor thy daughter, thy man-servant, nor thy maid-servant, nor thy cattle, nor the stranger that is within thy gates.

For in six days the Lord made heaven and earth, the sea, and all that in them is, and rested the seventh day: wherefore the Lord blessed the Sabbath-day and hallowed it.

V Honor thy father and thy mother; that thy days may be long upon the land which the Lord thy God giveth thee.

VI. Thou shalt not kill.

VII. Thou shalt not commit adultery.

VIII. Thou shalt not steal.

IX. Thou shalt not bear false witness against thy neighbor.

X. Thou shalt not covet thy neighbor's house; thou shalt not covet thy neighbor's wife, nor his man-servant, nor his maid-servant, nor his ox, nor his ass, nor any thing that is thy neighbor's.

And all the people saw the thunderings and the lightnings, and the noise of the trumpet, and the mountain smoking.

Heavenly Rest.

There is an hour of peaceful rest,
 To mourning wanderers given;
There is a tear for souls distressed,
A balm for every wounded breast;
 'Tis found above,—in heaven.

There is a soft, a downy bed,
 Fair as the breath of even;
A couch for weary mortals spread,
Where they may rest the aching head,
 And find repose,—in heaven.

There is a home for weary souls,
 By sin and sorrow driven;
When tossed on life's tempestuous shoals,
Where storms arise, and ocean rolls,
 And all is dark,—but heaven.

There fragrant flowers immortal bloom,
 And joys supreme are given.
There rays divine, disperse the gloom;
Beyond the confines of the tomb,
 Appears the dawn—of heaven.

All for the Best.

There was once an Eastern traveller, who always said that what God allowed to be done, was all for the best.

One day, he was wandering through a barren country, and

as night approached, he found himself very weary and hungry. The clouds, too, were growing black, as if a storm was coming. At last, he saw a village, and rode up to it, and asked for shelter and lodging for the night. But the men all refused, and drove him away; and he was obliged to go to the woods near by.

The poor traveller thought it was very hard that the people of the village should be so inhospitable to him; but he said God is just, and it is all for the best.

He turned his horse loose, so that he might eat some grass. He then lighted his lamp, and sat down under a tree, and began to read the book of the law. He had not read more than one chapter, when the storm burst upon him, and extinguished his lamp. He was very sorry that he had to stop reading, and to sit there in the dark without any thing to interest him. But he still said that it was all for the best.

After awhile, he stretched himself on the ground, with his faithful dog watching over him, and tried to go to sleep. But he had hardly closed his eyes, when a great wolf came, and killed his dog. "Alas," he said, "who will henceforth watch over me when I sleep? My trusty dog is gone! But, no doubt, it is all for the best."

Soon after he had said this, a lion came and devoured his horse. "What am I to do now?" said the poor man. "My lamp is out, and my dog is gone; and now my horse, too, is taken from me. But God knows what is best for us, poor mortals. It is all for the best."

He passed a sleepless night, and early next morning, went to the village to see if he could buy another horse, that he might pursue his journey. But what was his surprise, when he found that there was not a live person in the whole village! A band of robbers had come during the night, and killed all the people, and plundered their houses.

The traveller raised his voice in thanks to God, for having preserved him from the danger into which he was so near falling. "Now I know truly," he said, "that men are short-sighted and blind; often considering those things as evils, which God designs for their good. If the people had not been unkind to me, and driven me away from their village, I, too, should have been murdered by the robbers. If the wind had not put out my lamp, they would have found me under the tree, and killed me. And if my dog and my horse had

not been taken from me, their noise would have attracted the
attention of the robbers, and guided them to me. Blessed be
the name of the Lord, all is for the best."

The Rose.

The rose had been washed, just washed in a shower,
   Which Mary to Anna conveyed;
The plentiful moisture encumbered the flower,
   And weighed down its beautiful head.

The cup was all filled, and the leaves were all wet;
   And it seemed, to a fanciful view,
To weep for the buds it had left with regret,
   On the flourishing bush where it grew.

I hastily seized it, unfit as it was
   For a nosegay, so dripping and drowned;
And swinging it rudely, too rudely alas,
   I snapped it—it fell to the ground.

And such, I exclaimed, is the pitiless part,
   Some act by the delicate mind;
Regardless of wringing and breaking a heart,
   Already to sorrow resigned.

This elegant rose, had I shaken it less,
   Might have bloomed with its owner awhile;
And the tear that is wiped with a little address,
   May be followed, perhaps, by a smile.

The Good Boy.

The good boy loves his parents very dearly. He always
minds what they say to him, and tries to please them. If they
desire him not to do a thing, he does it not: if they desire
him to do a thing, he does it cheerfully.

When they deny him what he wishes for, he does not
grumble, or pout out his lips, or look angry: but he thinks,

that his parents know what is proper for him better than he does, because they are wiser than he is.

He loves his teachers, and all who tell him what is good. He likes to read, and to write, and to learn something new every day. He hopes that if he shall live to be a man, he shall know a great many things, and be very wise and good.

He is kind to his brothers and sisters, and all his little play-fellows. He never fights them, nor quarrels with them, nor calls them names. When he sees them do wrong, he is sorry, and tries to persuade them to do better.

He does not speak rudely to any body. If he sees any persons who are lame, or crooked, or very old, he does not laugh at them, nor mock them; but he is glad when he can do them any service.

He is kind even to dumb creatures: for he knows that though they cannot speak, they can feel as well as we. Even those animals which he does not think pretty, he takes care not to hurt.

He likes very much to see the birds pick up bits of hay, and moss, and wool, to build their nests with; and he likes to see the hen sitting on her nest, or feeding her young ones; and to see the little birds in their nest, and hear them chirp.

Sometimes he looks about in the bushes, and in the trees, and amongst the strawberry plants, to find nests: but when he has found them, he only peeps at them; he would rather not see the little birds, than frighten them, or do them any harm.

He never takes any thing that does not belong to him, or meddles with it without leave. When he walks in his father's garden, he does not pull flowers, or gather fruit, unless he is told that he may do so.

He never tells a lie. If he has done any mischief, he confesses it, and says he is very sorry, and will try to do so no more.

When he lies down at night, he tries to remember all he has been doing and learning in the day. If he has done wrong, he is sorry, and hopes he shall do so no more; and that God, who is so good, will love and bless him. He loves to pray to God, and to hear and read about Him; and to go with his parents and friends to worship Him.

Every body that knows this good boy loves him, and speaks well of him, and is kind to him; and he is very happy.

The Good Girl.

The industrious little girl always minds what her father and mother say to her; and she takes pains to learn whatever they are so kind as to teach her. She is never noisy or troublesome; so that they like to have her with them, and to talk to her, and to instruct her.

She has learned to read so well, and she is so good a girl, that her father has given her several little books, which she reads in by herself, whenever she likes; and she understands all that is in them.

She knows the meaning of a great many difficult words; and also the names of a great many countries, cities, and towns, and she can find them upon a map.

She can spell almost every little sentence, that her father asks her to spell; and she can write very prettily, even without a copy; and she can do a great many sums on a slate.

Whatever she does, she takes care to do it well; and when she is doing one thing, she tries not to think of another. If she has made a mistake, or done any thing wrong, she is sorry for it; and when she is told of a fault, she endeavors to avoid it another time.

When she wants to know any thing, she asks her father or mother to tell her; and she tries to understand, and to remember what they tell her; but if they do not think proper to answer her questions, she does not tease them, but says, "When I am older, they will perhaps instruct me," and she thinks about something else.

She likes to sit by her mother, and sew, or knit. When she sews, she does not take long stitches, or pucker her work; but does it very neatly, just as her mother tells her to do.— And she always keeps her work very clean; for if her hands are soiled, she washes them before she begins her work; and when she has finished it, she folds it up, and puts it by very carefully, in her work-bag, or in a drawer.

It is but very seldom, indeed, that she loses her thread or needles, or any thing she has to work with. She keeps her needles and thread in her little case; and she has a pincushion in which she puts her pins.

She takes care of her own clothes; and folds them up very neatly. She knows exactly where she puts them; and, she could find them even in the dark.

When she sees a hole in her frock, or any of her clothes, she mends it, or asks her mother to have it mended. She does not wait till the hole is very large, for she remembers what her mother has told her, that "A stitch in time saves nine."

She does not like to waste anything. She never throws away or burns crumbs of bread, or peelings of fruit, or little bits of muslin, or linen, or ends of thread; for she has seen the chickens and the little birds picking up crumbs, and the pigs feeding upon peelings of fruit; and she has seen the rag-man going about gathering rags, which, her mother has told her, he sells to people who make paper of them.

When she goes with her mother into the kitchen and the dairy, she takes notice of every thing she sees; but she does not meddle with any thing without leave. She knows how puddings, tarts, butter, and bread are made.

She can iron her own clothes, and she can make her own bed. She likes to feed the chickens and the young turkeys, and to give them clean water to drink and to wash themselves in. She likes to work in her little garden, to weed it, and to sow seeds and plant roots in it; and she likes to do little jobs for her mother, and be useful.

If all little girls would be so attentive and industrious, how they would delight their parents, and their kind friends; and they would be much happier themselves, than when they are obstinate, or idle, or ill-humored, and not willing to learn any thing properly, or mind what is said to them.

Elegy on Madame Blaize.

Good people, all, with one accord,
    Lament for Madam Blaize;
Who never wanted a good word,
    From those who spoke her praise.

The needy seldom passed her door,
    And always found her kind;
She freely lent to all the poor,
    Who left a pledge behind.

She strove the neighborhood to please,
  With manners wondrous winning;
She never followed wicked ways,
  Unless when she was sinning.

At church, in silks and satins new,
  With hoops of monstrous size,
She never slumbered in her pew,
  But when she shut her eyes.

Her love was sought, I do aver,
  By twenty beaux, or more;
The king himself hath followed her,
  When she has walked before.

But now, her wealth and finery fled,
  Her hangers-on, cut short all,
Her doctors found, when she was dead
  Her last disorder, mortal.

Let us lament, in sorrow sore;
  For Kent-street well may say,
That, had she lived a twelve-month more,
  She had not died to-day.

Description of Heaven.

And I saw a new heaven and a new earth; for the first heaven and the first earth were passed away, and there was no more sea.

And I, John, saw the holy city, new Jerusalem, coming down from God out of heaven, prepared as a bride adorned for her husband.

And I heard a great voice out of heaven, saying, Behold the tabernacle of God is with men, and he will dwell with them, and they shall be his people, and God himself shall be with them, and be their God.

And God shall wipe away all tears from their eyes; and there shall be no more death, neither sorrow, nor crying, neither shall there be any more pain: for the former things are passed away.

And the twelve gates were twelve pearls; every several gate was of one pearl; and the street of the city was pure gold, as it were transparent glass.

And I saw no temple therein; for the Lord God Almighty, and the Lamb, are the temple of it.

And the city had no need of the sun, neither of the moon, to shine it; for the glory of God did lighten it, and the Lamb is the light thereof.

And the gates of it shall not be shut at all by day; for there shall be no night there.

And there shall in no wise enter into it any thing that defileth, neither whatsover worketh abomination or maketh a lie; but they which are written in the Lamb's book of life.

The Dangers of Life.

Awake, my soul! lift up thine eyes;
See where thy foes against thee rise,
In long array, a num'rous host!
Awake my soul! or thou art lost.

Here giant danger, threat'ning stands,
Must'ring his pale, terrific bands;
There, pleasure's silken banners spread,
And willing souls are captive led.

See where rebellious passions rage,
And fierce desires and lusts engage:
The meanest foe of all the train
Has thousands and ten thousands slain.

Thou tread'st upon enchanted ground;
Perils and snares beset thee round;
Beware of all, guard every part,
But most the traitor in thy heart.

Come then, my soul, now learn to wield
The weight of thine immortal shield;
Put on the armor from above
Of heavenly truth and heavenly love.

The terror and the charm repel, .
And powers of earth, and powers of hell:
The man of Calv'ry triumph'd here ;
Why should his faithful followers fear? ˊ

The Good Samaritan.

And behold, a certain lawyer stood up and tempted Jesus,
saying, Master, what shall I do to inherit eternal life ?

Jesus said unto him, What is written in the law ?   How
readest thou ?

And he, answering, said, Thou shalt love the Lord thy God
with all thy heart, and with all thy soul, and with all thy
strength, and with all thy mind; and thy neighbor as thyself.

And Jesus said unto him, Thou hast answered right : this
do, and thou shalt live.

But he, willing to justify himself, said unto Jesus, And
who is my neighbor ?

And Jesus, answering, said, A certain man went down
from Jerusalem to Jericho, and fell among thieves, who
stripped him of his raiment, and wounded him, and departed,
leaving him half dead.

And by chance there came down a certain priest that way;
and when he saw him, he passed by on the other side.

And likewise a Levite, when he was at the place, came and
looked on him, and passed by on the other side.

But a certain Samaritan, as he journeyed, came where he
was : and when he saw him, he had compassion on him,

And went to him, and bound up his wounds, pouring in
oil and wine, and set him on his own beast, and brought him
to an inn, and took care of him.

And on the morrow, when he departed, he took out two
pence, and gave them to the host, and said unto him, Take
care of him; and whatsoever thou spendest more, when I
come again I will repay thee.

Which now of these three, thinkest thou, was neighbor
unto him that fell among the thieves ?

And he said, He that showed mercy on him. Then said
Jesus unto him, Go, and do thou likewise.

The Ant and the Glow-Worm.—A Fable.

When night had spread its darkest shade,
And even the stars no light conveyed,
A little ant of modest gait,
Was pacing homeward, somewhat late.

Rejoiced was she, to keep in sight,
A brilliant glow-worm's useful light;
Which, like a lantern clear, bestowed
Its brightness o'er her dangerous road.

Passing along with footstep firm,
She thus addressed the glittering worm :
" A blessing, neighbor, on your light !
I kindly thank you for it.   Good-night."

" What !" said the vain, though glowing thing,
" Do you employ the light I fling ?
I do not shine for such as you !"
It proudly then its light withdrew.

Just then a traveller, passing by,
Who had beheld with curious eye,
The beauteous brightness, now put out,
Left all in darkness and in doubt,
Unconscious stepped his foot aside,
And crushed the glow-worm in its pride.

God, in His wise and bounteous love,
Has given us talents to improve ;
And those who hide the precious store,
May do much harm, and suffer more.

————

Crucifixion of Christ.

And as they led Jesus away, they laid hold upon Simon, a
Cyrenian, coming out of the country, and on him they laid the
cross, that he might bear it after Jesus.

And there followed him a great company of people, and of women, which also bewailed and lamented him.

But Jesus turning unto them, said, Daughters of Jerusalem, weep not for me, but weep for yourselves, and for your children.

And there were also two others, malefactors, led with him to be put to death.

And when they were come to the place which is called Calvary, there they crucified him, and the malefactors; one on the right hand and the other on the left.

Then said Jesus, Father, forgive them, for they know not what they do. And they parted his raiment, and cast lots.

And the people stood beholding. And the rulers also with them derided him, saying, He saved others; let him save himself, if he be Christ, the chosen of God.

And the soldiers also mocked him, coming to him and offering him vinegar,

And saying, If thou be the King of the Jews, save thyself.

And a surperscription was also written over him, in letters of Greek, and Latin, and Hebrew, THIS IS THE KING OF THE JEWS.

And one of the malefactors which were hanged, railed on him, saying, If thou be Christ, save thyself and us.

But the other answering, rebuked him, saying, Dost thou not fear God, seeing thou art in the same condemnation?

And we indeed justly; for we receive the due reward of our deeds: but this man hath done nothing amiss.

And he said unto Jesus, Lord, remember me when thou comest into thy kingdom.

And Jesus said unto him, Verily I say unto thee, To-day shalt thou be with me in Paradise.

And it was about the sixth hour, and there was a darkness over all the earth until the ninth hour.

And the sun was darkened, and the vail of the temple was rent in the midst.

And when Jesus had cried with a loud voice, he said, Father, into thy hands I commend my spirit; and having said thus, he gave up the ghost.

Now when the centurion saw what was done, he glorified God, saying certainly this was a righteous man.

The Wise Bird and the Foolish Ones.—A Fable.

Once, on a morning in winter, the sun shone brightly, and the air was as mild and warm as if it were the month of June. The sun had melted the snow away, and the buds had almost begun to appear on the trees.

The little birds assembled in the grove, and some of them said that the spring had come, and that it was time to choose their mates and build their nests.

But there was an old bird who advised them not to be so fast. He told them that he had seen many such warm days in winter, before the cold weather was past. He said that the snow and the frost would come again, and that the weather would be too cold for them to build their nests.

"Wait a little while," said the wise old bird; "wait a little longer, until the winter is past, with its snow and its ice, and until the weather has become settled and warm."

While the old bird was talking, up jumped a pert young gold-finch. He had a smooth head, that shone like satin, and bright and beautiful wings; and he thought that he was very wise.

He told the other birds not to mind what the old bird said. He declared that he knew that the winter was over; and that, for his part, he intended to choose his mate, and build his nest, without waiting any longer.

Many of the other birds, said they would do so too. So they built their nests, and laid their eggs, and thought they were getting along ever so finely. But the old birds remained quiet, waiting for settled weather.

Soon the cold winds began to blow once more. The rain, and the hail, and the snow, fell again, and filled the nests with water and ice. The eggs were all spoiled, and the young birds now saw that they behaved in a very silly manner; and they said they would listen the next time to the advice of the wise old birds instead of those who had no experience.

The Boasting Girl and the Conceited Pigeon.

Anna Strong was a great boaster. She always wanted a very long lesson, and would say, "Indeed I can learn it all; it is not too hard for me." But when she went to recite it to her teacher, she very often knew nothing about it.

4

If any thing was to be done at home, or at school, Anna would always say, "*I* know how; please let *me* do it;" even if it was a thing she could not do at all.

One day, her teacher asked some one in the class, to point out some cities on the map, so that all in the class might see them. Anna jumped up, and asked the teacher to let her do it, for that she could do it very accurately.

The teacher gave consent, and Anna went to the map; but she could not find a single city that the teacher asked for.—So the teacher told her she was like the silly pigeon that the fable tells about.

The fable says that when the pigeon first came into the world, the other birds went to her, and offered to teach her how to build a nest. The robin showed her its nest, made of straw and mud; the cat-bird showed one made of sticks and bark; and the sparrow told how it had made its nest of hair and moss.

But the pigeon walked about in a very conceited manner, tossing her head from one side to the other, and said to the birds, "you need not tell *me*; *I* know how to build a nest as well as any of you."

The black-bird, and the dove, then offered their assistance, and told the pigeon how they made their nests. But the pigeon would hardly listen to them, but kept saying, "*I* know how."

At last, the birds all went away, and left her; but when the pigeon attempted to build her nest, she found that she knew nothing at all about it. And so she would not have had a nest at all, if men had not taken pity on her, and built her a pigeon-house, and put some hay in it.

When the teacher told her this fable, little Anna said that it is much better to be willing and anxious to learn, than to be boastful, and to pretend to know more than we do.

The Hare and the Tortoise.

Said a hare to a tortoise, "Good sir, what a while
You have been only crossing the way;
Why I really believe that to go half a mile,
You must travel two nights and a day."

"I am very contented," the creature replied,
 "Though I walk but tortoise's pace;
But if you think proper the point to decide,
   We will run half a mile in a race."

"Very good," said the hare; said the tortoise "Proceed,
   And the fox shall decide who has won;"
Then the hare started off with incredible speed;
   But the tortoise walk'd leisurely on.

"Come, tortoise, friend tortoise, walk on," said the hare,
   "While I shall stay here for my dinner;
Why, 'twill take you a month, at that rate, to get there,
   Then how can you hope to be winner?"

But the tortoise could not hear a word that she said,
   For he was far distant behind;
So the hare felt secure whilst at leisure she fed,
   And took a sound nap when she dined.

So at last this slow walker came up with the hare,
   And there fast asleep did he spy her;
And he cunningly crept with such caution and care,
   That she woke not, although he pass'd by her.

"Well now," thought the hare, when she open'd her eyes,
   "For the race—and I soon shall have done it;"
But who can describe her chagrin and surprise,
   When she found that the *tortoise* had won it?

Thus plain plodding people, we often shall find,
Will leave hasty confident people behind.

The Echo.

A little boy who had learned to bark like a dog, was one
day walking near a body of woods, when he thought he would
amuse himself by barking. So he said, "Bow! wow! wow!"
   As soon as he had made these sounds, a voice in the woods
said "Bow! wow! wow!" The little boy thought there was
a dog in the woods, and so he called out, "Doggy! doggy!"

As soon as he had said this he heard a voice in the woods say "Doggy! doggy!"

"Who are you?" said the little boy. "Who are you?" answered the voice in the woods. "I am named Edmund Blair," said the little boy. "I am named Edmund Blair," said the voice in the woods.

"What do you mock me for?" asked Edmund. "What do you mock me for?" was the answer which came back to him.

"If I can find you I will whip you," said Edmund. "If I can find you I will whip you," was the answer which quickly came back from the woods.

This so frightened Edmund, that he ran home, and told his father that there was a bad boy in the woods, who had threatened to whip him. His father laughed and told him that the bad boy was named Echo.

Edmund's father then explained to him; that when sound goes from us, and strikes a hard body, like a tree, or a wall, or a bank, it comes back to us, just as a ball does, if we throw it against a house-side. When the sound thus returns to us, we hear our own words over again, and this is called echo.

Edmund was no longer frightened after his father told him what it was that answered him, and so he went back, and amused himself a long time, talking to his echo.

The Little Lord and the Farmer's Boy.

A little lord, engaged in play,
Carelessly threw his ball away;
So far beyond the brook it flew,
His lordship knew not what to do.

It chanced there passed a farmer's boy,
Whistling a tune in childish joy;
His frock was patched, and his hat was old,
But the farmer's heart was very bold.

"You little chap! pick up my ball!"
His saucy lordship loud did call—

He thought it useless to be polite
To one whose clothes were in such a plight.

"Do it yourself, for want of me,"
The boy replied right manfully;
Then quietly he passed along,
Whistling aloud his fav'rite song.

His little lordship furious grew—
For he was proud and hasty too.
"I'll break your bones!" he rudely cries,
While fire was flashing from his eyes.

And heedless quite what steps he took,
He tumbled plump into the brook;
And as he fell, he dropped his bat,
And next he lost his beaver hat.

Come, help me out!" enraged he cried—
But the sturdy farmer thus replied:
"Alter your tone, my little man,
And then I'll help you all I can—

"There are few things I would not dare
For gentlemen, who speak me fair;
But for rude words I do not choose
To tire my feet and wet my shoes."

"Please help me," then his lordship said;
"I'm sorry I was so ill-bred."
"'Tis all forgot," replied the boy,
And gave his hand with honest joy.

The proffered aid his lordship took,
And soon came safely from the brook;
His looks were downcast and aside,
For he felt ashamed of his silly pride.

The farmer brought his ball and bat,
And wiped the wet from his drowning hat;
And he mildly said, as he went away,
"Remember the lesson you've learned to-day."

"Be kind to all you chance to meet
In field, or lane, or crowded street;
Anger and pride are both unwise—
Vinegar never catches flies."

Against Persecution.—A Parable.

And it came to pass after these things, that Aram sat in the door of his tent, about the going down of the sun.

And behold, a man, bowed with age, came from the way of the wilderness, leaning upon a staff.

And Aram arose, and went to meet him, and said unto him, Turn in I pray thee, and wash thy feet, and tarry all night, and thou shalt arise early on the morrow, and go thy way.

And the man said, Nay, for I will abide under this tree. But Aram pressed him greatly; so he turned, and they went into the tent; and Aram baked unleavened bread, and they did eat.

And when Aram saw that the man blessed not God, he said unto him, Wherefore dost thou not give thanks, and worship the most High God, Creator of heaven and earth?

And the man answered and said, I do not worship the God thou speakest off, neither do I call upon his name; for I have made me a god which abideth in my house, and provideth me with all things.

And Aram's zeal was kindled against the man, and he arose and fell upon him, and drove him forth, with blows, into the wilderness.

And at midnight, Aram heard the voice of the Lord, saying, Aram, where is the stranger that came unto thy tent?

And Aram answered and said, Lord, he would not worship thee, neither would he call upon thy name; wherefore have I driven him out from before my face, with blows, into the wilderness.

And God said, Have I not borne with him a hundred and ninety and eight years, and nourished him, and clothed him, notwithstanding he hath rebelled against me, and couldst not thou, that art thyself a sinner, bear with him one night?

And Aram said, Let not the anger of the Lord wax hot

against his servant; for, lo, I have sinned. And Aram arose, and went forth into the wilderness, and sought diligently for the man, and found him, and brought him to his tent; and he treated him kindly and did set meat before him, and he did eat. And when the morrow came, he sent him away, with gifts for his journey.

The Prodigal Son.

A certain man had two sons; and the younger of them said to his father, Father, give me the portion of goods that falleth to me. And he divided unto them his living.

Not many days after, the younger son gathered all together, and took his journey into a far country, and there wasted his substance in riotous living.

And when he had spent all, there arose a mighty famine in that land; and he began to be in want.

And he went and joined himself to a citizen of that country; and he sent him into his fields to feed swine.

And he would fain have filled himself with the husks that the swine did eat; and no man gave unto him.

And when he came to himself, he said, How many hired servants of my father's have bread enough and to spare, and I perish with hunger!

I will arise, and go to my father, and will say unto him, Father, I have sinned against heaven and before thee,

And am no more worthy to be called thy son: make me as one of thy hired servants.

And he arose and came to his father. But when he was yet a great way off, his father saw him, and had compassion, and ran and fell on his neck, and kissed him.

And the son said unto him, Father, I have sinned against heaven, and in thy sight, and am no more worthy to be called thy son.

But the father said to his servants, Bring forth the best robe, and put it on him; and put a ring on his hand, and shoes on his feet:

And bring hither the fatted calf, and kill it; and let us eat and be merry.

For this my son, was dead, and is alive again; he was lost and is found. And they began to be merry.

The Better Land.

" I hear thee speak of the better land ;
Thou call'st its children a happy band :
Mother! oh, where is that radiant shore ?
Shall we not seek it, and weep no more ?
Is it where the flower of the orange blows,
And the fire-flies glance through the myrtle boughs?"
" Not there, not there, my child !"

Is it where the feathery palm-trees rise,
And the date grows ripe under sunny skies ?
Or 'midst the green islands of glittering seas,
Where fragrant forests perfume the breeze ;
And strange, bright birds, on their starry wings,
Bear the rich hues of all glorious things ?"
" Not there, not there, my child !"

" Is it far away in some region old,
Where the rivers wander o'er sands of gold ?
Where the burning rays of the ruby shine,
And the diamond lights up the secret mine,
And the pearl gleams forth from the coral strand,—
Is it there, sweet mother, that better land ?"
" Not there, not there, my child !"

" Eye hath not seen it, my gentle boy ;
Ear hath not heard its deep sounds of joy ;
Dreams cannot picture a world so fair ;
Sorrow and death may not enter there ;
Time doth not breathe on its fadeless bloom ;
For beyond the clouds and beyond the tomb,
It is there, it is there, my child !"

How to Make the Best of It.

Robinet, a peasant of Lorraine, in France, was hastening
home after a hard day's work, with a little basket of provi-
sions in his hand. " What a delicious supper I shall have !"
said he to himself. This piece of kid, well stewed down,
with my onions sliced, thickened with my meal, and seasoned

with my salt and pepper, will make a dish fit for the bishop of the diocese. Then I have a good piece of barley-loaf at home, to finish with. How I long to be at it."

A noise close by, now attracted his notice, and he spied a squirrel nimbly running up a tree, and popping into a hole between the branches. "Ha!" thought he, "what a nice present a nest of young squirrels will be to my little master. I'll try if I can get it."

Upon this, he set down his basket in the road, and began to climb the tree. He had half ascended, when casting a look at his basket, he saw a dog with his nose in it, ferretting out the piece of kid's flesh. He made all possible speed down, but the dog was too quick for him, and ran off with the meat in his mouth. Robinet could only look after him. "Well," said he, "then I must be contented with soup-maigre,—and no bad thing either."

He travelled on, and came to an inn on the road-side, where an acquaintance was sitting, who invited him to stop. Robinet took a seat on the bench, and set his basket close by him. A tame raven, which was kept at the house, came slyly behind him, and stole away the bag in which the meal was tied up, and hopped off with it to his hole.

Robinet did not miss the bag until he had started on his journey again. He then returned to search for it, but could hear no tidings of it. "Well," says he, "my soup will be the thinner; but I will boil a slice of bread in it, and that will do some good at least."

He went on again, and arrived at a little brook, over which was laid a narrow plank. A young woman coming up to pass at the same time, Robinet politely offered her his hand, to assist her. As soon as she got to the middle, either through fear or sport, she cried out that she was falling. Robinet, hastening to support her with his other hand, let his basket drop into the stream.

As soon as he had conducted her safely over, Robinet jumped into the water, and recovered his basket; but when he took it out, he perceived that all the salt was melted, and the pepper washed away. Nothing was now left but the onions. "Well," says Robinet, "then I must sup to-night on roasted onions and barley-bread. Last night I had the bread alone. To-morrow morning it will not signify what I had." So saying, he trudged on, singing as cheerfully as ever.

The Discontented Mole.—A Fable.

A young mole having crept out into the sun one day, met with its mother, and began to complain of its lot. "I have been thinking," said he, "that we lead a very stupid life, burrowing under the ground, and dwelling in perpetual darkness. For my part, I think it would be much better to live above-board, and caper about in the sunlight like the squirrels."

"It may seem so to you," said the wise old mole, "but beware of forming hasty opinions. It is an old remark, that it takes all sorts of people to make a world. Some creatures live upon the trees; but nature has provided them with claws, which make it easy and safe for them to climb. Some dwell in the water; but they are supplied with fins, which render it easy for them to move about, and with a contrivance by means of which they breathe where other creatures would drown.

"Some creatures glide through the air; but they are endowed with wings, without which, it would be vain to attempt to fly. The truth is, that every individual is made to fill some place in the scale of being; and he best seeks his own happiness in following the path which his Creator has marked out for him.

"We may wisely seek to better our condition, by making that path as pleasant as possible, but not attempt to pursue one which we are unfitted to follow. You will best consult your interest, by endeavoring to enjoy all that properly belongs to a mole, instead of striving to swim like a fish, climb like a squirrel, or fly like a bird. Contentment is the great blessing of life. You may enjoy this in the quiet security of your sheltered abode; the proudest tenant of the earth, air, or sea, can do no more."

The young mole replied: "This may seem very wise to you, but it sounds like nonsense to me. I am determined to burrow in the earth no more, but dash out in style, like other gay people." So saying, he crept upon a little mound for the purpose of looking about, and seeing what course of pleasure he should adopt. While in this situation, he was snapped up by a hawk, who carried him to a tall tree, and devoured him without ceremony.

This fable teaches us to be contented with our lot. We

should patiently perform the duties of the position in which we are placed, and be satisfied with the pleasures and advantages which Providence has placed within our reach.

The Eyes and the Nose.

Between Nose and Eyes, a strange contest arose;
   The spectacles set them, unhappily, wrong.
The point in dispute was, as all the world knows,
   To which the said spectacles ought to belong.

So Tongue was the lawyer, and argued the cause,
   With a great deal of skill, and a wig full of learning;
While Chief Baron Ear sat to balance the laws,
   So famed for his talent in nicely discerning.

"In behalf of the Nose, it will quickly appear,
   And your lordship," he said, " will undoubtedly find,
That the Nose has had spectacles always to wear,
   Which amounts to possession, time out of mind."

Then holding the spectacles up to the court,—
   " Your lordship observes, they are made with a straddle,
As wide as the ridge of the nose is; in short,
   Designed to sit close to it, just like a saddle.

"Again, would your lordship, a moment, suppose,
   ('Tis a case that has happened, and may be again,)
That the visage or countenance had not a nose,—
   Pray who would, or could, wear spectacles then?

"On the whole it appears, and my argument shows,
   With a reasoning the court will never condemn,
That the spectacles plainly were made for the Nose,
   And the Nose was as plainly intended for them."

Then shifting his side, (as a lawyer knows how,)
   He pleaded again in behalf of the Eyes.
But what were his arguments, few people know,
   For the court did not think they were equally wise.

So his lordship decreed, with a grave, solemn tone,
  Decisive and clear, without one *if* or *but*,—
That whenever the Nose put the spectacles on,
  By daylight or candle light,—Eyes should be shut.

The French Youth

A youth who had been admitted into a military school in France, soon attracted the attention of his comrades by his great abstemiousness. Although a variety of food was placed upon the table, he never partook of any thing but bread and soup, and drank nothing but water.

His teacher being informed of the conduct of the youth, ascribed it to mistaken devotion, and gave him a reproof. But the youth persisted in his course, and it was finally brought to the knowledge of the superintendent of the school.

The superintendent brought the boy before him, and gently informed him that such singularity of conduct excited remark, and produced disorder, and was by no means proper in a public instution; and he told him he must conform to the rules and the diet of the school.

The superintendent then inquired of the youth his reason for acting in the manner he had done; but the latter was unwilling to answer. The superintendent, at last, threatened that if he still persisted in his refusal to explain himself, he should be compelled to return him home again to his family. This menace had the desired effect, and the youth then disclosed the motive of his conduct.

"You will not, I hope, be displeased with me, sir," said he; "but I could not bring myself to enjoy what I think luxury, while I reflect that my dear father and mother, are in the utmost indigence. They could afford themselves and me no better food than coarse brown bread, and of that, but very little. Here, I have excellent soup, and an abundance of good white bread. The recollection of the situation in which I left my parents, would not permit me to indulge myself by eating any thing else."

The superintendent could not restrain his tears, at such an instance of filial love and sensibility. "Has not your father been in the military service," he inquired. "Why, then, has he no pension?" "For want of friends and money, sir," replied the youth. "He waited upon the government, seeking for a pension, until his money became exhausted; and rather than contract debts, he is content to languish in the manner I have told you."

"Well," said the superintendent, "if the facts are as you have stated them, I will be a friend to your father. I will undertake to procure his pension for him. In the mean time, here are three pieces of gold for yourself, as a present from the king; and I will send your father a month's pay in advance, out of the pension which I am sure of obtaining for him."

"How can you send the money to him?" asked the boy. "Let that give you no uneasiness," replied the superintendent. "I shall find a way." "Ah, sir," said the boy with eagerness, "if you can send it so easily, will you be kind enough to send him also these three pieces of gold, which you were so good as to give me? Here I am in want of nothing; and they will be of the greatest service to my father, in assisting him to provide for my brothers and sisters."

The Battle of Blenheim.

It was on a summer evening,
  Old Kaspar's work was done,
And he, before his cottage door,
  Was sitting in the sun;
And by him sported on the green,
His little grandchild Wilhelmine.

She saw her brother Peterkin
  Roll something large and round,
Which he beside the rivulet,
  In playing there, had found;
He came to ask what he had found,
That was so large, and smooth, and round.

Old Kaspar took it from the boy,
  Who stood expectant by;
And then the old man shook his head,
  And with a natural sigh,
"'Tis some poor fellow's skull," said he,
"Who fell in the great victory."

"I find them in the garden,
    For there's many here about;
And often when I go to plough,
    The ploughshare turns them out;
For many thousand men," said he,
"Were slain in that great victory."

"Now tell us what 'twas all about,"
    Young Peterkin, he cries;
While little Wilhelmine looks up,
    With wonder-waiting eyes;
"Now tell us all about the war,
And what they killed each other for."

"It was the English," Kaspar cried,
    "Who put the French to rout,
But what they killed each other for,
    I could not well make out.
But every body said," quoth he,
"That 'twas a famous victory.

"My father lived at Blenheim then,
    Yon little stream, hard by;
They burnt his dwelling to the ground,
    And he was forced to fly;
So, with his wife and child, he fled,
Nor had he where to rest his head.

"With fire and sword, the country round
    Was wasted, far and wide;
And many a nursing mother then,
    And new-born baby died;
But things like that, you know, must be
At every famous victory.

"They say it was a shocking sight
    After the field was won;
For many thousand bodies here
    Lay rotting in the sun;
But things like that, you know, must be
After a famous victory.

"Great praise the Duke of Marlbro' won,
And our young prince, Eugene."
"Why, 'twas a very wicked thing!"
Said little Wilhelmine,
"Nay, nay, my little girl," quoth he,
"It was a famous victory.

"And every body praised the Duke,
Who this great fight did win."
"But what good came of it at last?"
Quoth little Peterkin.
"Why, that I cannot tell," said he,
"But 'twas a glorious victory."

The Day of Judgment.

When the Son of man shall come in his glory, and the holy angels with him, then shall he sit upon the throne of his glory:

And before him shall be gathered all nations; and he shall separate them one from another, as a shepherd divideth his sheep from the goats:

And he shall set the sheep on his right hand, but the goats on the left.

Then shall the King say unto them on his right hand, Come, ye blessed of my Father, inherit the kingdom prepared for you from the foundation of the world:

For I was an hungered, and ye gave me meat: I was thirsty, and ye gave me drink: I was a stranger, and ye took me in:

Naked, and ye clothed me: I was sick, and ye visited me: I was in prison, and ye came unto me.

Then shall the righteous answer him, saying, Lord, when saw we thee an hungered, and fed thee? or thirsty, and gave thee drink?

When saw we thee a stranger, and took thee in? or naked, and clothed thee?

Or when saw we thee sick, or in prison, and came unto thee?

And the King shall answer and say unto them, Verily, I

say unto you, Inasmuch as ye have done it unto one of the least of these my brethren, ye have done it unto me.

Then shall he also say unto them on the left hand, Depart from me, ye cursed, into everlasting fire, prepared for the devil and his angels:

For I was an hungered, and ye gave me no meat: I was thirsty, and ye gave me no drink: I was a stranger, and ye took me not in: or naked, and ye clothed me not: sick and in prison, and ye visited me not.

Then shall they also answer him, saying, Lord, when saw we thee an hungered, or athirst, or a stranger, or naked, or sick, or in prison, and did not minister unto thee?

Then shall he answer them, saying, Verily, I say unto you, Inasmuch as ye did it not to one of the least of these, ye did it not to me.

And these shall go their way into everlasting punishment: but the righteous into life eternal.

The Doomed Man.

There is a time, we know not when,
　A point we know not where,
That marks the destiny of men
　To glory or despair.

There is a line, by us unseen,
　That crosses every path;
The hidden boundary between
　God's patience and his wrath.

To pass that limit is to die,
　To die as if by stealth;
It does not quench the beaming eye,
　Or pale the glow of health.

The conscience may be still at ease,
　The spirit light and gay,
That which is pleasing, still may please,
　And care be thrust away.

But on that forehead God has set
    Indelibly a mark;
Unseen by man, for man as yet,
    Is blind and in the dark.

And yet the doomed man's path below,
    Like Eden may have bloomed,
He did not, does not, will not know,
    Or feel that he is doomed.

He knows, he feels that all is well,
    And every fear is calmed;
He lives, he dies, he wakes in hell,
    Not only doomed, but damned.

O, where is this mysterious bourn,
    By which our path is crossed;
Beyond which, God himself has sworn,
    That he who goes, is lost!

How far may we go on in sin?
    How long will God forbear?
Where does hope end, and where begin
    The confines of despair?

An answer from the sky is sent,
    Ye that from God depart,
While it is called to-day repent,
    And harden not your heart.

The Whistle.

"When I was a child of seven years old," says Dr. Franklin, "my friends, on a holyday, filled my pocket with halfpence.

"I went directly towards a shop where toys for children were sold; and being charmed with the sound of a whistle that I met by the way, in the hands of another boy, I voluntarily offered him all my money for it.

"Then I came home, and went whistling over the house, much pleased with my whistle, but disturbing all the family. My brothers, and sisters, and cousins, understanding the bargain I had made, told me I had given four times as much for it as it was worth.

"This put me in mind what good things I might have bought with the rest of my money, and they laughed at me so much for my folly, that I cried with vexation. My reflections on the subject gave me more chagrin, than the whistle gave me pleasure.

"This little event, however, was afterwards of use to me, the impression continuing on my mind : so that often, when I was tempted to buy some unnecessary thing, I said to myself, 'Do not give too much for the whistle;' and so I saved my money.

"As I grew up, came into the world, and observed the actions of men, I thought I met with many, very many, who gave too much for the whistle.

"When I saw any one too ambitious of court-favor, sacrificing his time in attendance on levees, his repose, his liberty, his virtue, and perhaps his friends, to attain it, I have said to myself, 'This man gives too much for his whistle.'

"When I saw another fond of popularity, constantly employing himself in political bustles, neglecting his own affairs, and ruining them by that neglect : 'He pays indeed,' said I, 'too much for his whistle.'

"If I knew a miser, who gave up every kind of comfortable living, all the pleasures of doing good to others, all the esteem of his fellow-citizens, and the joys of benevolent friendship, for the sake of accumulating wealth : 'Poor man !' said I, 'you indeed pay too much for your whistle.'

"When I met a man of pleasure, sacrificing every laudable improvement of mind, or of fortune, to mere sensual gratifications : 'Mistaken man,' said I, 'you are providing pain for yourself, instead of pleasure ; you give too much for your whistle.'

"If I saw one fond of fine clothes, fine furniture, fine equipages, all above his fortune, for which he contracted debts, and ended his career in prison : 'Alas !' said I, 'he has paid dear, very dear, for his whistle.'

"In short, I conceived that great part of the miseries of mankind, were brought upon them by the false estimate they had made of the value of things, and by their giving too much for their whistles."

My Life is like the Summer Rose.

My life is like the summer rose,
    Which opens to the morning sky,
But, ere the shades of evening close,
    Are scattered on the ground to die,
Yet on the rose's humble head
The softest dews of night are shed,
As though she wept such waste to see—
But none shall shed one tear for me.

My life is like the autumn leaf,
    That trembles in the moon's pale ray :
Its hold is frail, its date is brief,
    Restless, and soon to pass away.
Yet, when that leaf shall fall and fade,
The parent tree shall mourn its shade ;
The winds bewail the leafless tree—
But none shall breathe one sigh for me.

My life is like the print of feet
    Left on Tampa's desert strand ;
Soon as the rising tide shall beat,
    All trace shall vanish from the sand.
Yet, as grieving to efface
All vestige of the human race,
On that lone shore loud moans the sea—
But none shall thus lament for me.

Industry Rewarded

A rich husbandman had two sons, the one exactly a year der than the other. The very day the second was born, he t, in the entrance of his orchard, two young apple-trees of qual size, which he cultivated with the same care, and which grew so equally, that no person could perceive the least difference between them.

When his children were capable of handling garden tools, he took them, one fine morning in spring, to see these two trees, which he had planted for them, and called after their names; and when they had sufficiently admired their growth, and the number of blossoms that covered them, he said:

"My dear children, I give you these trees; you see they are in good condition. They will thrive as much by your care, as they will decline by your negligence; and their fruit will reward you in proportion to your labor."

The youngest, named Edmund, was industrious and attentive. He busied himself in clearing his tree of insects that would hurt it; and he propped up its stem, to prevent its taking a wrong bent.

He loosened the earth about it, that the warmth of the sun, and the moisture of the dews, might cherish the roots. His mother had not tended him more carefully in his infancy, than he tended his young apple-tree.

His brother, Moses, did not imitate his example. He spent a great deal of time on a mount that was near, throwing stones at the passengers in the road. He went among all the little dirty country boys in the neighborhood, to box with them; so that he was often seen with broken shins and black eyes, from the kicks and blows he received in his quarrels.

In short, he neglected his tree so far, that he never thought of it, till one day in autumn he by chance saw Edmund's tree so full of apples streaked with purple and gold, that had it not been for the props which supported its branches, the weight of its fruit must have bent it to the ground.

Struck with the sight of so fine a tree, he hastened to his own, hoping to find as large a crop upon it; but, to his great surprise, he saw scarcely any thing, except branches covered with moss, and a few yellow withered leaves.

Full of passion and jealousy, he ran to his father, and said: "Father, what sort of a tree is that which you have given me? It is as dry as a broomstick; and I shall not have ten apples on it. My brother you have used better: bid him at least share his apples with me."

"Share with you!" said his father; "so the industrious must lose his labor, to feed the idle! Be satisfied with your lot: it is the effect of your negligence; and do not think to accuse me of injustice, when you see your brother's rich crop. Your tree was as fruitful, and in as good order as his; it bore as many blossoms, and grew in the same soil, only it was not fostered with the same care.

"Edmund has kept his tree clear of hurtful insects; but you have suffered them to eat up yours in its blossoms. As I do not choose to let any thing which God has given me, and for which I hold myself accountable to Him, go to ruin, I shall take this tree from you, and call it no more by your name.

"It must pass through your brother's hands, before it can recover itself; and from this moment, both it and the fruit it may bear are his property. You may, if you will, go into my nursery, and look for another, and rear it, to make amends for your fault; but if you neglect it, that too shall be given to your brother, for assisting me in my labor."

Moses felt the justice of his father's sentence, and the wisdom of his design. He, therefore, went that moment into the nursery, and chose one of the most thriving apple-trees he could find. Edmund assisted him with his advice in rearing it; and Moses embraced every occasion of paying attention to it.

He was now never out of humor with his comrades, and still less with himself; for he applied himself cheerfully to work; and in autumn, he had the pleasure of seeing his tree fully answer his hopes. Thus he had the double advantage, of enriching himself with a splendid crop of fruit, and at the same time of subduing the vicious habits he had contracted. His father was so well pleased with this change, that the following year he divided the produce of a small orchard between him and his brother.

The Fall of the Leaf.

See the leaves around ye falling,
　Dry and wither'd, to the ground,
Thus to thoughtless mortals calling,
　In a sad and solemn sound:

"Sons of Adam, once in Eden,
　Whence like us he blighted fell,

Hear the lecture we are reading,
  'Tis, alas! the truth we tell.

"Virgins, much, too much presuming,
  On your boasted white and red,
View us, late in beauty blooming,
  Number'd now among the dead.

"Griping misers, nightly waking,
  See the end of all your care;
Fled on wings of our own making,
  We have left our owners bare.

"Sons of honor, fed on praises,
  Flutt'ring high in fancied worth,
Lo, the fickle air that raises,
  Brings us down to parent earth.

"Learned sires, in systems jaded,
  Who for new ones daily call,
Cease, at length, by us persuaded,
  Every leaf must have a fall.

"Youth, yet no losses grieve you,
  Gay in health and many a grace,
Let not cloudless skies deceive you,
  Summer gives to Autumn place.

"On the tree of life eternal,
  Man, let all thy hopes be stay'd,
Which alone, forever vernal,
  Bears the leaves that never fade."

Mungo Park's Travels in Africa.

I waited more than two hours, without having an opportunity of crossing the river; during which time the people, who had crossed, carried information to Mansong, the king, that a white man was waiting for a passage, and was coming to see him.

He immediately sent over one of his chief men, who informed me that the king could not possibly see me, until he knew what had brought me into his country, and that I must not presume to cross the river without the king's permission.

He, therefore, advised me to lodge at a distant village, to which he pointed, for the night; and said that, in the morning, he would give me further instructions how to conduct myself.

This was very discouraging. However, as there was no remedy, I set off for the village, where I found, to my great mortification, that no person would admit me into his house.

I was regarded with astonishment and fear, and was obliged to sit all day, without victuals, in the shade of a tree; and the night threatened to be very uncomfortable, for the wind rose and there was great appearance of a heavy rain; and the wild beasts are so very numerous in the neighborhood, that I should have been under the necessity of climbimg up the tree, and resting among the branches.

About sunset, however, as I was preparing to pass the night in this manner, and had turned my horse loose that he might graze at liberty, a woman returning from the labors of the field, stopped to observe me, and perceiving that I was weary and dejected, inquired into my situation, which I briefly explained to her; whereupon, with looks of great compassion, she took up my saddle and bridle, and told me to follow her.

Having conducted me into her hut, she lighted up a lamp, spread a mat on the floor, and told me I might remain there for the night. Finding that I was very hungry, she said she would procure me something to eat. She accordingly went out, and returned in a short time with a very fine fish, which, having caused to be half broiled upon some embers, she gave me for supper.

The rights of hospitality being thus performed towards a stranger in distress, my worthy benefactress, pointing to the mat, and telling me I might sleep there without apprehension, called to the female part of her family, who had stood gazing on me all the while in fixed astonishment, to resume their task of spinning cotton, in which they continued to employ themselves great part of the night.

They lightened their labors by songs, one of which was composed extempore, for I was myself the subject of it. It

was sung by one of the young women, the rest joining in a
sort of chorus. The air was sweet and plaintive, and the
words, literally translated, were these :

"The winds roared and the rains fell. The poor white
man, faint and weary, came and sat under our tree. He has
no mother to bring him milk; no wife to grind him corn.
Chorus—Let us pity the white man; no mother has he to
bring him milk ; no wife to grind him corn."

Trifling as this recital may appear to the reader, to a person
in my situation, the circumstance was affecting in the highest
degree ; I was oppressed by such unexpected kindness, and
sleep fled from my eyes. In the morning, I presented my
compassionate landlady with two of the four brass buttons
which remained on my waistcoat, the only recompense I could
make her.

The song of the negroes, above related, has been turned
into the following verses by the Duchess of Devonshire :

> The loud wind roar'd, the rain fell fast;
> The white man yielded to the blast;
> He sat him down beneath our tree,
> For weary, sad, and faint was he ;
> And, ah ! no wife nor mother's care,
> For him the milk or corn prepare.
>
> CHORUS.
>
> The white man shall our pity share ;
> Alas ! no wife nor mother's care,
> For him the milk or corn prepare.
>
> The storm is o'er, the tempest past,
> And Mercy's voice has hush'd the blast :
> The wind is heard in whispers low ;
> The white man far away must go ;
> But ever in his heart will bear
> Remembrance of the negro's care.
>
> CHORUS.
>
> Go, white man, go—but with thee bear
> The negro's wish, the negro's prayer,
> Remembrance of the negro's care.

The Wonderful Chip.

The following narrative, by Mr. Williams, missionary to Rarotonga, describes, in a striking manner, the feelings of an untaught people, when observing for the first time the effects of written communications.

"In the erection of my chapel," says he, "having come to the work one morning without my square, I picked up a chip, and with a piece of charcoal wrote upon it a request that Mrs. Williams would send me that article.

"I called a chief, who was superintending a part of the work, and said to him, 'Friend, take this; go to our house, and give it to Mrs. Williams.'

"He was a singular looking man, remarkably quick in his movements, and had been a great warrior; but, in one of the numerous battles he had fought, he had lost an eye; and, giving me an inexpressible look with the other, he said: 'Take that! She will call me a fool, and scold me, if I carry a chip to her.' 'No,' I replied, 'she will not; take it and go immediately; I am in haste.'

"Perceiving me to be in earnest, he took it, and asked, 'What must I say?' I replied, 'You have nothing to say; the chip will say all I wish.'

"With a look of astonishment and contempt, he held up the piece of wood, and said. 'How can this speak? Has this a mouth?' I desired him to take it immediately, and not spend so much time talking about it.

"On arriving at the house, he gave the chip to Mrs. Williams, who read it, threw it away, and went to the tool chest. The chief, resolved to see the result of this mysterious proceeding, followed her closely. On receiving the square from her he said, 'Stay, daughter; how do you know that it is this what Mr. Williams wants?'

"'Why,' she replied, 'did you not bring me a chip just now?' 'Yes,' said the astonished warrior, 'but I did not hear it say anything.' 'If you did not, I did,' was the reply, 'for it made known to me what he wanted; and all you have to do is to return with it as quickly as possible.'

"With this the chief leaped out of the house, and, catching up the mysterious piece of wood, he ran through the settlement with the chip in one hand, and the square in the other, holding them up as high as his hands would reach, and shout-

5

ing as he went, 'See the wisdom of these English people!
They can make chips talk! They can make chips talk!'

"On giving me the square, he wished to know how it was
possible thus to converse with persons at a distance. I gave
him all the explanation in my power; but it was a circumstance involved in so much mystery, that he actually tied a
string to the chip, hung it around his neck, and wore it for
some time.

"During several days, we frequently saw him, surrounded
by a crowd, who were listening with intense interest, while he
narrated the wonders the chip had performed."

A Pleasant Surprise.

A young man of eighteen or twenty, a student in a univer-
sity, took a walk one day with a professor, who was commonly
called the student's friend, such was his kindness to the young
men whom it was his office to instruct. While they were
walking together, and the professor was seeking to lead the
conversation to grave subjects, they saw a pair of old shoes
lying in their path, which they supposed to belong to a poor
man who was at work close by, and who had nearly finished
his day's task.

The young student turned to the professor, saying, "Let us
play the man a trick; we will hide his shoes, and conceal ourselves behind those bushes, and watch his perplexity when he
cannot find them." "My dear friend," answered the professor, "we must never amuse ourselves at the expense of the
poor. But you are rich, and you may give yourself a much
greater pleasure by means of this poor man. Put a dollar into
each shoe, and then we will hide ourselves."

The student did so, and then placed himself, with the professor, behind the bushes close by, through which they could
easily watch the laborer, and see whatever wonder or joy he
might express. The poor man soon finished his work, and
came across the field to the path, where he had left his coat
and shoes. While he put on the coat, he slipped one foot
into one of his shoes; but, feeling something hard, he stooped
down and found the dollar. Astonishment and wonder were
seen upon his countenance. He gazed upon the dollar, turned

it around, and looked again and again; then he looked around him on all sides, but could see no one.

He put the money in his pocket, and then proceeded to put on the other shoe; but how great his surprise when he found the other dollar! His feelings overcame him. He saw that the money was a present, and he fell upon his knees, looked up to heaven, and uttered aloud a fervent thanksgiving, in which he spoke of his wife sick and helpless, and his children without bread, whom this timely bounty from some unknown hand, would save from perishing.

The young man was deeply affected, and tears filled his eyes. "Now," said the professor, "are you not much better pleased than if you had played your intended trick?" "O, dearest sir," answered the youth, "you have taught me a lesson that I will never forget! I feel now the truth of the words, which I never before understood, 'It is better to give than to receive.' We should never approach the poor but with the wish to do them good."

The Spider and the Fly.—A Fable.

"Will you walk into my parlor?" said a spider to a fly;
"'Tis the prettiest little parlor that ever you did spy.
The way into my parlor is up a winding stair,
And I have many pretty things to show you when you are
    there."
"Oh no, no," said the little fly, "to ask me is in vain,
For who goes up your winding stair can ne'er come down
    again."

"I'm sure you must be weary with soaring up so high;
Will you rest upon my little bed?" said the spider to the fly,
"There are pretty curtains drawn around, the sheets are fine
    and thin;
And if you like to rest awhile, I'll snugly tuck you in."
"Oh no, no," said the little fly, "for I've often heard it said,
They never, never, wake again, who sleep upon your bed."

Said the cunning spider to the fly, "Dear friend, what shall
    I do,
To prove the warm affection I have always felt for you?

I have within my pantry, good store of all that's nice;
I'm sure you're very welcome; will you please to take a slice?"
"Oh no, no." said the little fly; "kind sir, that cannot be;
I have *heard* what's in your pantry, and I do not *wish* to see."

"Sweet creature," said the spider, "you're witty and you're
    wise,
How handsome are your gauzy wings, how brilliant are your
    eyes!
I have a little looking-glass, upon my parlor shelf,
If you'll step in one moment, dear, you shall behold yourself."
"I thank you, gentle sir," she said, "for what you are pleased
    to say;
And bidding you good morning now, I'll call another day."

The spider turned him round about, and went into his den,
For well he knew the silly fly would soon be back again,
So he wove a secret web, in a little corner sly,
And set his table ready to dine upon the fly.
Then he went out to his door again, and merrily did sing,
"Come hither, hither, pretty fly, with the pearl and silver wing:
Your robes are green and purple; there's a crest upon your
    head;
Your eyes are like the diamond bright, but mine are dull as
    lead."

Alas, alas! how very soon this silly little fly,
Hearing his wily, flattering words. came slowly flitting by;
With buzzing wings she hung aloft; then near and nearer
    drew,
Thinking only of her brilliant eyes, and green and purple
    hue;
Thinking only of her crested head—*poor foolish thing!* At
    last,
Up jumped the cunning spider, and fiercely held her fast!

He dragged her up his winding stair, into his dismal den,
Within his little parlor; but she never came out again!
And now my dear young friends, who may this story read,
To idle, silly, flattering words, I pray you ne'er give heed;
Unto an evil counsellor, close heart, and ear, and eye,
And take a lesson from the tale of the Spider and the Fly.

The Lion.

The lion is a native of the warmest climates. He is found in the greatest numbers in the desolate regions of the torrid zone, and in all the interior parts of the vast continent of Africa, and the hottest parts of Asia.

In those desert regions, whence mankind are driven by the rigorous heat of the climate, this animal reigns sole master. His disposition seems to partake of the ardor of his native soil. Inflamed by the influence of a burning sun, his rage is most terrible, and his courage undaunted.

From many accounts, we are assured, that, powerful and terrible as this animal appears, his anger is noble, his courage magnanimous, and his temper susceptible of grateful impressions.

The lion has often been seen to despise weak and contemptible enemies, and even to disregard their insults, when it was in his power to punish them.

He has been known to spare the life of an animal which was thrown into his den to be devoured by him, to live in habits of perfect cordiality with it, to suffer it to partake of his subsistence, and even to give it a preference when his portion of food was scanty.

The form of the lion is strikingly bold and majestic. His large and shaggy mane, which he can erect at pleasure, surrounding his awful front; his huge eye-brows; his round and fiery eye-balls, which, upon the least irritation, seem to glow with peculiar lustre; together with the formidable appearance of his teeth, exhibit a picture of terrific grandeur, which is difficult to be expressed.

The length of the largest lion is between eight and nine feet; the tail about four; and his height about four feet and a half. The female is about one-fourth part less, and without a mane.

The roaring of the lion is loud and dreadful. When heard in the night, it resembles distant thunder. His cry of anger is much shriller and shorter.

The lion seldom attacks any animal openly, except when impelled by extreme hunger; and in that case, no danger deters him. But, as most animals endeavor to avoid him, he is obliged to have recourse to artifice, and take his prey by surprise.

For this purpose, he crouches in some thicket, where he waits till his prey approaches; and then, with a prodigious spring, he leaps upon it like a cat, and generally seizes it at the first bound.

His lurking places are generally near a spring, or by the side of a river, where he has frequently an opportunity of catching such animals as come to quench their thirst.

As a proof that the lion is capable of exercising a generous and friendly disposition towards mankind, and especially towards his keeper, we have the following account of an incident which happened in Paris in the year 1799.

Citizen Felix, who kept two lions, a male and a female, in the national menagerie, was taken ill, and could no longer attend to feed them, but another person was obliged to do his office.

The lion appeared sad and solitary; and remained from that time constantly seated at the end of the cage, and refused to receive anything from the stranger.

His presence was hateful to him; and he menaced him by bellowing. The company even of the female seemed to displease him, and he paid little or no attention to her. The uneasiness of the animal afforded a belief that he was really ill, but no one durst approach him.

At length Felix recovered of his illness, and intending to surprise the lion, he went softly to the cage, and showed the lion only his face against the bars. As soon as the lion discovered him, he leaped against the side of the cage, patted Felix with his paws, licked his hands and face, and seemed to tremble with pleasure.

The female also ran to him, but the lion drove her back, seemed angry, and fearful she should snatch any favors from Felix. A quarrel seemed about to take place between them, but Felix entered the cage to pacify them, and caressed them by turns.

Felix has frequently been seen in the midst of this formidable couple, whose power he has fettered by kindness. If he wishes that they should separate and retire to their respective cages, he has only to speak a word, and they obey.

If he wishes that they should lie down, and show strangers their paws, armed with frightful claws, and their throats full of tremendous teeth, at his command they lie on their backs, hold up their paws one after another, and open their mouths: and as a recompense, obtain the favor of licking his hand.

These two animals, at the time of this incident, were said to be five years and a half old, of a strong breed, both of the same lioness, and have always lived together.

The Cuckoo.

Hail, beauteous stranger of the grove,
  Thou messenger of Spring!
Now Heaven repairs thy rural seat,
  And woods thy welcome sing.

What time the daisy decks the green,
  Thy certain voice we hear.
Hast thou a star to guide thy path,
  Or mark the rolling year?

Delightful visitant, with thee
  I hail the time of flowers,
And hear the sound of music sweet,
  From birds among the bowers.

The school-boy wandering through the wood,
  To pull the flowers so gay,
Starts the new voice of Spring to hear,
  And imitates thy lay.

What time the pea puts on the bloom,
  Thou flyest the vocal vale;
An annual guest in other lands,
  Another Spring to hail.

Sweet bird, thy bower is ever green,
  Thy sky is ever clear;
Thou hast no sorrow in thy song,
  No winter in thy year!

Oh, could I fly, I'd fly with thee;
  We'd make with joyful wing,
Our annual visit o'er the globe,
  Companions of the Spring.

The Chinese Prisoner.

A certain emperor of China, on his accession to the throne of his ancestors, commanded a general release of all those who were confined in prison for debt. Among that number, was an old man, who had fallen an early victim to adversity, and whose days of imprisonment, reckoned by the notches he had cut on the door of his gloomy cell, expressed the annual circuit of more than fifty suns.

With trembling hands and faltering steps, he departed from his mansion of sorrow; his eyes were dazzled with the splendor of light, and the face of nature presented to his view a perfect paradise The jail in which he had been imprisoned stood at some distance from Pekin, and to that city he directed his course, impatient to enjoy the caresses of his wife, his children, and his friends.

Having with difficulty found his way to the street in which his decent mansion had formerly stood, his heart became more and more elated at every step he advanced. With joy he proceeded, looking eagerly around; but he observed few of the objects with which he had been formerly conversant. A magnificent edifice was erected on the site of the house which he had inhabited; the dwellings of his neighbors had assumed a new form; and he beheld not a single face of which he had the least remembrance.

An aged beggar, who, with trembling limbs, stood at the gate of an ancient portico, from which he had been thrust by the insolent domestic who guarded it, struck his attention. He stopped, therefore, to give him a small pittance out of the amount of the bounty with which he had been supplied by the emperor, and received, in return, the sad tidings that his wife had fallen a lingering sacrifice to penury and sorrow; that his children were gone to seek their fortunes in distant or unknown climes; and that the grave contained his nearest and most valued friends.

Overwhelmed with anguish, he hastened to the palace of his sovereign, into whose presence his hoary locks and mournful visage soon obtained him admission; and, casting himself at the feet of the emperor, "Great Prince," he cried, "send me back to that prison from which mistaken mercy has delivered me! I have survived my family and friends, and even in the midst of this populous city, I find myself in a dreary solitude.

The cell of my dungeon protected me from the gazers at my wretchedness, and whilst secluded from society, I was the less sensible of the loss of its enjoyments. I am now tortured with the view of pleasure in which I cannot participate; and die with thirst, though streams of delight surround me."

Signs of Rain.

The hollow wind begins to blow;
The clouds look black; the glass is low;
The soot falls down; the spaniels sleep;
And spiders from their cobwebs peep.

Hark! how the chairs and tables crack!
Old Betty's joints are on the rack;
Loud quack the ducks; the peacocks cry;
The distant hills are seeming nigh.

How restless are the snorting swine!
The busy flies disturb the kine;
Low o'er the grass the swallow wings;
The cricket, too, how sharp he sings!

Puss on the hearth, with velvet paws,
Sits wiping o'er her whiskered jaws.
'Twill surely rain: I see, with sorrow,
Our jaunt must be put off to-morrow.

Heroism of a Peasant.

A great inundation having taken place in the north of Italy, caused by an excessive fall of snow on the Alps, followed by a speedy thaw, the river Adige carried off a bridge near Verona, except the middle part of it, on which was the house of the toll-gatherer or porter, who, with his family, thus remained imprisoned by the waves, and in momentary danger of destruction.

They were discovered from the banks, stretching forth their hands, screaming and imploring succor, while fragments of the remaining arch continually dropped into the water.

In this danger, a nobleman, who was present, held ont a purse of one hundred sequins, as a reward to any adventurer, who would take a boat and deliver this unhappy family.

But the risk of being borne down by the rapidity of the stream, of being dashed against the fragments of the bridge, or of being crushed by the falling stones, was so great, that not one of the vast numbers of spectators had courage enough to attempt such an enterprise.

A peasant, who was passing along at this juncture, being informed of the proposed reward, immediately jumped into a boat, and by strength of oars gained the middle of the river, and brought his boat under the pile, where the whole family descended into it by means of a rope.

"Courage!" exclaimed he, "now you are safe." By a still more strenuous effort, and great strength of arm, through Divine Providence, he brought the boat and family safe to shore.

"Brave fellow," exclaimed the nobleman, handing the purse to him, "here is the promised recompense."

"I shall never expose my life for money," replied the peasant. "My labor is sufficient to procure a livelihood for myself, my wife and children; give the purse to this poor family, who have lost all."

The Meeting of the Waters.

There is not in the wide world, a valley so sweet,
As that vale in whose bosom the bright waters meet.
O, the last rays of feeling and life must depart,
Ere the bloom of that valley shall fade from my heart.

Yet it was not that nature had shed o'er the scene,
Her purest of crystal and brightest of green;
'Twas not her soft magic of streamlet or hill;
O, no!—it was something more exquisite still.

'Twas that friends, the beloved of my bosom, were near,
Who made every dear scene of enchantment more dear;
And who felt how the best charms of nature improve,
When we see them reflected from looks that we love.

Sweet vale of Avoca! how calm could I rest
In thy bosom of shade, with the friends I love best!
Where the storms that we feel in this cold world should cease,
And our hearts, like thy waters, be mingled in peace.

The Resurrection and Ascension of Christ.

Now upon the first day of the week, very early in the morning, they came unto the sepulchre, bringing the spices which they had prepared, and certain others with them.

And they found the stone rolled away from the sepulchre;

And they entered in, and found not the body of the Lord Jesus.

And it came to pass, as they were much perplexed thereabout, behold, two men stood by them in shining garments:

And as they were afraid, and bowed down their faces to the earth, they said unto them, Why seek ye the living among the dead?

He is not here, but is risen: remember how he spake unto you when he was yet in Galilee,

Saying, the Son of Man must be delivered into the hands of sinful men, and be crucified, and the third day rise again.

And they remembered his words,

And returned from the sepulchre, and told all these things unto the eleven, and to all the rest.

It was Mary Magdalene, and Joanna, and Mary the mother of James, and other women that were with them, who told these things unto the apostles.

And their words seemed to them as idle tales, and they believed them not.

Then arose Peter, and ran unto the sepulchre; and stooping down, he beheld the linen clothes laid by themselves, and departed, wondering in himself at that which was come to pass.

And, behold, two of them went that same day to a village called Emmaus, which was from Jerusalem about threescore furlongs.

And they talked together of all these things which had happened.

And it came to pass, that, while they communed together and reasoned, Jesus himself drew near, and went with them.

But their eyes were holden that they should not know him.

And they drew nigh unto the village whither they went: and he made as though he would have gone further.

But they constrained him, saying, Abide with us: for it is toward evening, and the day is far spent. And he went in to tarry with them.

And it came to pass, as he sat at meat with them, he took bread, and blessed it, and brake, and gave to them.

And their eyes were opened, and they knew him; and he vanished out of their sight.

And they said one to another, Did not our heart burn within us, while he talked with us by the way, and while he opened to us the Scriptures?

And they rose the same hour, and returned to Jerusalem, and found the eleven gathered together, and them that were with them,

Saying, The Lord is risen indeed, and hath appeared to Simon.

And they told what things were done on the way, and how he was known of them in breaking of bread.

And as they thus spake, Jesus himself stood in the midst of them, and saith unto them, Peace be unto you.

But they were terrified and affrighted, and supposed they had seen a spirit.

And he said unto them, Why are ye troubled? and why do thoughts arise in your hearts?

Behold my hands and my feet, that it is I myself: handle me and see; for a spirit hath not flesh and bones, as ye see me have.

And when he had thus spoken, he showed them his hands and his feet.

And while they yet believed not for joy, and wondered, he said unto them, Have ye here any meat?

And they gave him a piece of a broiled fish, and of a honeycomb.

And he took it, and did eat before them,

And he led them out as far as Bethany; and he lifted up his hands and blessed them.

And it came to pass, while he blessed them, he was parted from them, and carried up into heaven.

And while they looked steadfastly toward heaven, as he went up, behold, two men stood by them in white apparel,

Who also said, Ye men of Galilee, why stand ye gazing up into heaven? This same Jesus who is taken up from you into heaven, shall so come in like manner as ye have seen him go into heaven.

Not Ashamed of Jesus.

Jesus! and shall it ever be,
A mortal man ashamed of thee?
Ashamed of thee, whom angels praise,
Whose glories shine through endless days?

Ashamed of Jesus! sooner far
Let evening blush to own her star:
He sheds the beams of Light Divine,
O'er this benighted soul of mine.

Ashamed of Jesus! just as soon,
Let midnight be ashamed of noon;
'Tis midnight with my soul till he,
Bright Morning Star, bid darkness flee!

Ashamed of Jesus! that dear Friend,
On whom my hopes of heaven depend?
No: when I blush, be this my shame,
That I no more revere his name.

Ashamed of Jesus! yes I may,
When I've no guilt to wash away;
No tears to wipe, no good to crave,
No fears to quell, no soul to save.

Till then,—nor is my boasting vain,
Till then I'll boast a Saviour slain.
And Oh! may this my glory be,
My Saviour not ashamed of me!

Ninetieth Psalm.

Lord, thou hast been our dwelling place in all generations.

Before the mountains were brought forth, or ever thou hadst formed the earth and the world, even from everlasting to everlasting, thou art God.

Thou turnest man to destruction; and sayest Return ye children of men.

For a thousand years in thy sight, are but as yesterday when it is past, and as a watch in the night.

Thou carriest them away as with a flood; they are as a sleep: in the morning they are like grass which groweth up.

In the morning it flourisheth, and groweth up; in the evening it is cut down, and withereth.

For we are consumed by thine anger, and by thy wrath are we troubled.

Thou hast set our iniquities before thee, our secret sins in the light of thy countenance.

For all our days are passed away in thy wrath; we spend our years as a tale that is told.

The days of our years are threescore years and ten; and if by reason of strength they be fourscore years, yet is their strength labor and sorrow: for it is soon cut off, and we fly away.

Who knoweth the power of thine anger? even according to thy fear, so is thy wrath.

So teach us to number our days, that we may apply our hearts unto wisdom.

Return O Lord, how long? and let it repent thee concerning thy servants.

O satisfy us early with thy mercy; that we may rejoice and be glad all our days.

Make us glad according to the days wherein thou hast afflicted us, and the years wherein we have seen evil.

Let thy work appear unto thy servants, and thy glory unto their children.

And let the beauty of the Lord our God be upon us: and establish thou the work of our hands upon us; yea, the work of our hands establish thou it.

Destruction of Sennacherib.

The Assyrian came down, like the wolf on the fold,
And his cohorts were gleaming in purple and gold;

And the sheen of their spears was like stars on the sea,
When the blue wave rolls nightly on deep Galilee.

Like the leaves of the forest when Summer is green,
That host, with their banners, at sunset was seen :
Like the leaves of the forest when Autumn hath blown,
That host, on the morrow, lay withered and strown.

For the angel of death spread his wings on the blast,
And breathed in the face of the foe as he passed ;
And the eyes of the sleepers waxed deadly and chill,
And their hearts but once heaved, and forever grew still.

And there lay the steed, with his nostril all wide,
But through it there rolled not the breath of his pride :
And the foam of his gasping lay white on the turf,
And cold as the spray of the rock-beating surf.

And there lay the rider, distorted and pale,
With the dew on his brow, and the rust on his mail ;
And the tents were all silent, the banners alone,
The lances unlifted, the trumpet unblown.

And the widows of Ashur, are loud in their wail,
And the idols are broke in the temple of Baal ;
And the might of the Gentile, unsmote by the sword,
Hath melted like snow, in the glance of the Lord !

Abraham's Plea in behalf of Sodom.

And the men rose up from thence, and looked toward Sodom : And Abraham went with them to bring them on the
way.

And the Lord said, Because the cry of Sodom and Gomor-
rah is great, and because their sin is very grievous ;

I will go down now, and see whether they have done alto-
gether according to the cry of it, which is come unto me;
and if not, I will know.

And the men turned their faces from thence, and went toward Sodom : but Abraham stood yet before the Lord.

And Abraham drew near, and said, Wilt thou also destroy
the righteous with the wicked ?

Peradventure there be fifty righteous within the city: wilt thou also destroy and not spare the place for the fifty righteous that are therein?

That be far from thee to do after this manner, to slay the righteous with the wicked; and that the righteous should be as the wicked, that be far from thee. Shall not the judge of all the earth do right?

And the Lord said, If I find in Sodom fifty righteous within the city, then I will spare all the place for their sakes.

And Abraham answered and said, Behold now, I have taken upon me to speak unto the Lord, who am but dust and ashes:

Peradventure there shall lack five of the fifty righteous: wilt thou destroy all the city for lack of five? And he said, If I find there forty and five, I will not destroy it.

And he spake yet again, and said, Peradventure there shall be forty found there. And he said, I will not do it for forty's sake.

And he said unto him, O let not the Lord be angry, and I will speak: Peradventure there shall thirty be found there. And he said, I will not do it if I find thirty there.

And he said, Behold now, I have taken upon me to speak unto the Lord: Peradventure there shall be twenty found there. And he said, I will not destroy it for twenty's sake.

And he said, O let not the Lord be angry, and I will speak yet but this once. Peradventure ten shall be found there. And he said, I will not destroy it for ten's sake.

And the Lord went his way, as soon as he had left communing with Abraham: And Abraham returned unto his place.

Turn the Carpet.

As at their work two weavers sat,
Beguiling time with friendly chat,
They touched upon the price of meat,
So high a weaver scarce could eat.
" What with my brats and sickly wife,"
Quoth Dick, " I'm almost tired of life;
So hard my work, so poor my fare,
'Tis more than mortal man can bear.

" How glorious is the rich man's state !
His house so fine ! his wealth so great !
Heaven is unjust, you must agree.
Why all to him ? why none to me ?
In spite of what the Scripture teaches,
In spite of all the parson preaches,
This world (indeed, I've thought so long)
Is ruled, methinks, extremely wrong.
Where'er I look, howe'er I range,
'Tis all confused, and hard, and strange ;
The good are troubled and oppressed,
And all the wicked are the blessed."

Quoth John, " Our ignorance is the cause
Why thus we blame our Maker's laws.
Parts of his ways alone we know ;
'Tis all that man can see below.
Seest thou that carpet, not half done,
Which thou, dear Dick, hast well begun ?
Behold the wild confusion there !
So rude the mass, it makes one stare.
A stranger, ignorant of the trade,
Would say, no meaning's there conveyed ;
For where's the middle ? where's the border ?
Thy carpet now is all disorder."

Said Dick, " My work is yet in bits,
But still in every part it fits ;
Beside, you reason like a lout ;
Why, man, that carpet's inside out !"
Says John. " Thou say'st the thing I mean ;
And now I hope to cure thy spleen.
This world, which clouds thy soul with doubt,
Is but a carpet inside out.

" As when we view these shreds and ends,
We know not what the whole intends,
So, when on earth things look but odd,
They re working still some scheme of God.
No plan, no pattern can we trace ;
All wants proportion. truth, and grace ;
The motley mixture we deride,
Nor see the beauteous upper side.

" But when we reach that world of light,
And view those works of God aright,
Then shall we see the whole design,
And own the Workman is Divine.
What now seem random strokes, will there
All order and design appear;
Then shall we praise what here we spurned;
For then *the carpet shall be turned!*"
"Thou'rt right," quoth Dick, " no more I'll grumble
That this sad world's so strange a jumble;
My impious doubts are put to flight,
For my own carpet sets me right."

---

*Judah's Supplication to Joseph for the Liberation of
Benjamin.*

Then Judah came near unto Joseph, and said, Oh, my
lord, let thy servant, I pray thee, speak a word in my lord's
ears, and let not thine anger burn against thy servant: for
thou art even as Pharaoh.

My lord asked his servants, saying, Have ye a father, or a
brother?

And we said unto my lord, We have a father, an old man,
and a child of his old age, a little one: and his brother is
dead, and he alone is left of his mother, and his father loveth
him.

And thou saidst unto thy servants, Bring him down unto
me, that I may set mine eyes upon him.

And we said unto my lord, The lad cannot leave his
father: for if he should leave his father, his father would
die.

And thou saidst unto thy servants, Except your youngest
brother come down with you, ye shall see my face no more.

And it came to pass, when we came up unto thy servant my
father, we told him the words of my lord.

And our father said, Go again, buy us a little food.

And we said, We cannot go down: if our youngest brother
be with us, then will we go down: for we may not see the
man's face except our youngest brother be with us.

And thy servant my father said unto us, Ye know that my
wife bare me two sons.

And the one went out from me, and I said, Surely he is torn in pieces; and I saw him not since:

And if ye take this also from me, and mischief befall him, ye shall bring down my gray hairs with sorrow to the grave.

Now, therefore, when I come to thy servant my father, and the lad be not with us; seeing that his life is bound up in the lad's life;

It shall come to pass, when he seeth that the lad is not with us, that he will die: and thy servants shall bring down the gray hairs of thy servant our father, with sorrow to the grave.

For thy servant became surety for the lad unto my father, saying, If I bring him not unto thee, then I shall bear the blame unto my father forever.

Now, therefore, I pray thee, let thy servant abide instead of the lad, a bondman to my lord; and let the lad go up with his brethren.

For how shall I go up to my father, and the lad be not with us? lest peradventure I see the evil that shall come on my father.

Joseph Makes Himself Known to his Brethren.

Then Joseph could not refrain himself before all them that stood by him; and he cried, Cause every man to go out from me. And there stood no man with him, while Joseph made himself known unto his brethren.

And he wept aloud: and the Egyptians and the house of Pharoah heard.

And Joseph said unto his brethren, I am Joseph: doth my father yet live? And his brethren could not answer him; for they were troubled at his presence.

And Joseph said unto his brethren, Come near to me, I pray you: and they came near. And he said, I am Joseph your brother, whom ye sold into Egypt.

Now, therefore, be not grieved nor angry with yourselves, that ye sold me hither; for God did send me before you to preserve life.

For these two years hath the famine been in the land; and yet there are five years in the which there shall be neither earing nor harvest.

And God sent me before you to preserve you a posterity in the earth, and to save your lives by a great deliverance.

So now, it was not you that sent me hither, but God: and he hath made me a father to Pharcah, and lord of all his house, and a ruler throughout all the land of Egypt.

Haste you, and go up to my father, and say unto him, Thus saith thy son Joseph, God hath made me lord of all Egypt: come down unto me, tarry not.

And thou shalt dwell in the land of Goshen, and thou shalt be near unto me, thou and thy children, and thy children's children, and thy flocks, and thy herds, and all that thou hast:

And there will I nourish thee, (for yet there are five years of famine,) lest thou, and thy household, and all that thou hast, come to poverty.

And behold your eyes see, and the eyes of my brother Benjamin, that it is my mouth that speaketh unto you.

And you shall tell my father of all my glory in Egypt, and of all that you have seen; and ye shall haste, and bring down my father hither

And he fell upon his brother Benjamin's neck and wept; and Benjamin wept upon his neck.

Moreover, he kissed all his brethren, and wept upon them; and after that, his brethren talked with him.

And the fame thereof was heard in Pharoah's house, saying, Joseph's brethren are come: and it pleased Pharoah well, and his servants.

And Pharoah said unto Joseph, Say unto thy brethren, This do ye; lade your beasts, and go, get you unto the land of Canaan;

And take your father, and your households, and come unto me; and I will give you the good of the land of Egypt, and ye shall eat the fat of the land.

Now thou art commanded, this do ye: Take your wagons out of the land of Egypt for your little ones, and for your wives, and bring your father, and come.

Also regard not your stuff: for the good of all the land of Egypt is yours.

And the children of Israel did so: and Joseph gave them wagons, according to the commandment of Pharoah, and gave them provision for the way.

And they went up out of Egypt, and came into the land of Canaan unto Jacob their father,

And told him, saying, Joseph is yet alive, and he is gover-

nor over all the land of Egypt. And Jacob's heart fainted,
for he believed them not

And they told him all the words of Joseph, which he had
said unto them: and when he saw the wagons which Joseph
had sent to carry him, the spirit of Jacob their father
revived.

And Israel said. It is enough: Joseph, my son, is yet alive;
I will go down and see him before I die.

The Sluggard.

'Tis the voice of the Sluggard: I heard him complain.
"You have waked me too soon I must slumber again."
As the door on its hinges, so he on his bed
Turns his sides, and his shoulders, and his heavy head.

"A little more sleep, and a little more slumber."
Thus he wastes half his days, and his hours without number;
And when he gets up, he sits folding his hands,
Or walks about sauntering, or trifling he stands.

I passed by his garden, and saw the wild brier,
The thorn, and the thistle grow broader and higher:
The clothes that hang on him are turning to rags;
And his money still wastes, till he starves or he begs.

I made him a visit, still hoping to find
He had taken better care for improving his mind:
He told me his dreams, talk'd of eating and drinking;
But he scarce reads his Bible, and never loves thinking.

Said I then to my heart, "Here's a lesson for me!
That man's but a picture of what I might be;
But thanks to my friends for their care in my breeding,
Who have taught me by times to love working and reading'"

The Tutor and his Pupils; Or, Use Your Eyes

Well, Robert, where have you been walking this afternoon?
said a tutor to one of his pupils at the close of a holiday.

Robert.—I have been to Broom-heath, and so round by the windmill upon Camp-mount, and home through the meadows by the river side.

Tutor.—Well, that is a pleasant round.

Robert.—I thought it very dull, sir; I scarcely met with a single person. I would much rather have gone along the turnpike road.

Tutor.—Why, if seeing men and horses is your object, you would, indeed, be better entertained on the high road. But did you see William?

Robert.—We set out together, but he lagged behind in the lane, so I walked on and left him.

Tutor.—That was a pity. He would have been company for you.

Robert —O! he is so tedious, always stopping to look at this thing and that; I would rather walk alone. I dare say he has not got home yet.

Tutor.—Here he comes. Well, William, where have you been?

William.—O, the pleasantest walk! I went all over Broom-heath, and so up to the mill at the top of the mount, and then down among the green meadows by the side of the river.

Tutor.—Why, that is just the round Robert has been taking; and he complains of its dullness, and prefers the high road.

William.—I wonder at that. I am sure I hardly took a step that did not delight me, and I have brought home my handkerchief full of curiosities.

Tutor.—Suppose, then, you give us an account of what amused you so much. I fancy it will be as new to Robert as to me.

William.—I will do it readily. The lane leading to the heath, you know, is close and sandy; so I did not mind it much, but made the best of my way; however, I spied a curious thing enough in the hedge. It was an old crab tree, out of which grew a great branch of something green, quite different from the tree itself. Here is a branch of it.

Tutor.—Ah! this is mistletoe; a plant of great fame for the use made of it by the Druids of old, in their religious rites and incantations. It bears a slimy white berry, of which bird-lime is made, whence its Latin name of *viscus.* It is one of those plants which do not grow in the ground by a root of their own, but **fix** themselves upon other plants; whence they have been humorously styled "parasitical," as being hangers-on or dependents. It was the mistletoe of the oak that the Druids particularly honored.

William.—A little further on I saw a green wood-pecker fly to a tree, and run up the trunk like a cat.

Tutor.—That was to seek for insects in the bark, on which they live. They bore holes with their strong bills for that purpose, and do much damage to the trees by it.

William.—When I got upon the open heath, how charming it was! The air seemed so fresh, and the prospect on every side so free and unbounded! Then it was all covered with gay flowers, many of which I had never observed before. There was a flock of lapwings upon a marshy part of the heath, that amused me much. As I came near them, some of them kept flying round and round, just over my head, and crying "pewit," so distinctly one might almost fancy they spoke. I thought I should have caught one of them, for he flew as if one of his wings was broken, and often tumbled close to the ground; but as I came near he always contrived to get away.

Tutor—Ha, ha! you were finely taken in, then! This was all an artifice of the bird's, to entice you away from its nest; for they build upon the bare ground, and their nest would easily be observed did they not draw off the attention of intruders by their loud cries and counterfeited lameness.

William.—I wish I had known that, for he led me a long chase, often over shoes in water. However, it was the cause of my falling in with an old man and a boy, who were cutting and piling up turf for fuel; and I had a good deal of talk with them about the manner of preparing the turf, and the price it sells at.

I then took my course up to the windmill, on the mount. I climbed up the steps of the mill, in order to get a better view of the country around. What an extensive prospect! I counted fifteen church steeples; and I saw several gentlemen's houses peeping out from the midst of green woods and plantations; and I could trace the windings of the river all along the low grounds, till it was lost behind a ridge of hills.

From the hill I went straight down to the meadows below, and walked on the side of a little brook till it entered the river, and then I took the path that runs along the bank. On the opposite side I observed several little birds running along the shore, and making a piping noise. They were brown and white, and about as big as a snipe.

Tutor—I suppose they were sand pipers—one of the numerous family of birds that get their living by wading among the shallows, and picking up worms and insects.

William.—There were a great many swallows, too, sporting on the surface of the water, that entertained me with their motions. Sometimes they dashed into the stream; sometimes they pursued one another so quickly that the eye could scarcely follow them. In one place, where a high, steep sand-bank rose directly above the river, I observed many of them go in and out of holes with which the bank was bored full.

Tutor—Those were sand martins, the smallest of our four species of swallows. They are of a mouse-color above and white beneath. They make their nests and bring up their young in these holes, which run a great depth, and by their situation are secure from all plunderers.

William.—A little further I saw a man in a boat, who was catching eels in an odd way. He had a long pole, with broad iron prongs at the end, just like Neptune's trident, only there were five instead of three This he pushed straight down among the mud in the deepest part of the river, and fetched up eels sticking between the prongs.

Tutor.—I have seen this method. It is called spearing of eels.

William.—While I was looking at him a heron came flying over my head with his large flagging wings. He alighted at the next turn of the river, and I crept softly behind the bank to watch his motions He had waded into the water as far as his long legs would carry him, and was standing with his neck drawn in, looking intently on the stream. Presently he dashed his long bill as quick as lightning into the water, and drew out a fish, which he swallowed. I saw him catch another in the same manner. He then took alarm at some noise I made, and flew away slowly to a wood at some distance, where he settled.

Tutor.—Probably his nest was there; for herons build upon the loftiest trees they can find, and sometimes in society together, like rooks. Formerly, when these birds were valued for the amusement of hawking, many gentlemen had their heronries; and a few are still remaining.

William.—I then turned homeward across the meadows,

where I stopped a while to look at a large flock of starlings, which kept flying about at no great distance. I could not tell at first what to make of them; for they rose all together from the ground as thick as a swarm of bees, and formed themselves into a kind of black cloud, hovering over the field. After taking a short round, they settled again, and presently rose again in the same manner. I dare say there were hundreds of them.

Tutor.—Perhaps so, for in the fenny countries their flocks are so numerous as to break down whole acres of reeds, by settling on them. This disposition of starlings to fly in close swarms, was remarked even by Homer, who compares the foe flying from one of his heroes, to a cloud of starlings retiring dismayed at the approach of the hawk.

William.—After I had left the meadows, I crossed the corn-fields in the way to our house, and passed close by a deep marl-pit. Looking into it, I saw in one of the sides, a cluster of what I took to be shells; and upon going down, I picked up a clod of marl, which was quite full of them: but how sea-shells could get there, I cannot imagine.

Tutor.—I do not wonder at your surprise, since many philosophers have been much perplexed to account for the same appearance. It is not uncommon to find great quantities of shells and relics of marine animals, even in the bowels of high mountains very remote from the sea.

William.—I got to the high field next to our house just as the sun was setting, and I stood looking at it till it was quite lost. What a glorious sight! The clouds were tinged with purple, and crimson, and yellow, of all shades and hues, and the clear sky varied from blue to a fine green at the horizon. But how large the sun appears just as it sets! I think it seems twice as big as when it is overhead.

Tutor—It does so; and you may probably have observed the same apparent enlargement of the moon at its rising.

William—I have; but pray what is the reason of this?

Tutor—It is an optical deception, depending upon principles which I cannot well explain to you, till you know more of that branch of science. But what a number of new ideas this afternoon's walk has afforded you! I do not wonder that you found it amusing; it has been very instructing, too. Did you see nothing of all these sights, Robert?

Robert.—I saw some of them, but I did not take particular notice of them.

6

Tutor.—Why not?

Robert.—I do not know. I did not care about them; and I made the best of my way home.

Tutor.—That would have been right if you had been sent on a message; but as you walked only for amusement, it would have been wiser to have sought out as many sources of it as possible. But so it is, one man walks through the world with his eyes open, and another with them shut; and upon this difference depends all the superiority of knowledge the one acquires above the other.

I have known a sailor who had been in all quarters of the world, and could tell you nothing but the signs of the tippling houses he frequented in different ports, and the price and quality of the liquor. On the other hand, a Franklin could not cross the English Channel without making some observations useful to mankind.

While many a vacant, thoughtless youth, is whirled throughout Europe, without gaining a single idea worth crossing a street for, the observing eye and inquiring mind, find matter for improvement and delight in every ramble in town or country. Do you, then, William, continue to make use of your eyes, and you, Robert, learn that eyes were given you to use.

What is That, Mother?

" What is that, mother ?"
            " The lark, my child.
The morn has just looked out and smiled,
When he starts from his humble, grassy nest,
And is up and away, with the dew on his breast,
And a hymn in his heart, to yon pure, bright sphere,
To warble it out in his Maker's ear.
Ever, my child, be thy morn's first lays
Tuned, like the lark's, to thy Maker's praise."

" What is that, mother ?"
            " The dove, my son;
And that low, sweet voice, like the widow's moan,
Is flowing out from her gentle breast,
Constant and pure by that lonely nest,

As the wave is poured from some crystal urn,
For her distant dear one's quick return.
Ever, my son, be thou like the dove ;
In friendship as faithful, as constant in love."

" What is that, mother ?"

"The eagle, my boy,
Proudly careering his course of joy ;
Firm, in his own mountain vigor relying ;
Breasting the dark storm ; the red bolt defying :
His wing on the wind, and his eye on the sun,
He swerves not a hair, but bears onward, right on.
Boy, may the eagle's flight ever be thine,
Onward, and upward, and true to the line."

" What is that, mother ?"

· " The swan, my love.
He is floating down from his native grove ;
No loved one now, no nestling nigh ;
He is floating down, by himself, to die.
Death darkens his eye, and unplumes his wings ;
Yet his sweetest song is the last he sings.
Live so, my love, that, when death shall come,
Swan-like and sweet it may waft thee home."

Little John and his Bowl of Milk

There was once a little boy by the name of John. He demeaned himself very well, and was generally of a good temper ; but he was too fond of his own pleasure, and would sometimes be unkind or uncivil, rather than deny himself an enjoyment, for the sake of doing a favor to another person.

One night when little John sat down to his supper, he asked for the bowl of milk which his kind mother always gave him at that meal. His mother told him he must do without milk that night ; for that a poor woman who lived close by, had sent to ask for some milk for her sick child, and she had given it all to her.

John did not behave like a good boy when his mother told him this. He pouted, and looked surly and angry ; and he said to his mother he did not like to have his milk given away to other children ; and that he would not eat his supper at all.

The good mother was very sorry to see her little son show such unconcern for the comfort of a sick person. But she told him, as he was so unwilling, she would never give his milk away again.

She thought, however, of a plan by which she hoped to lead her little boy to cherish better feelings. So the next morning, she told him, to get his hat and take a walk with her. John was always eager to go with his mother, for he loved her very much. So he got his hat, and ran to open the gate for her, and they were soon on their way.

The first place at which they stopped was the house where the little sick child lived ; and when they walked in, John's mother asked the lady how the child was. "Oh madam," said she, " little Charley is a great deal better this morning. That milk you sent him, acted like a charm ! It is the first thing he has eaten for two days. He begged for some, and I did not know where I could get any, except at your house. It was very kind of you to send it to him. As soon as he drank it, he fell asleep, and slept sweetly all night long ; and this morning he looks so much better that I feel as if my dear little boy would get well again."

John's mother told the lady she was very glad to hear that her little boy was so much better, and said she would like to send him some milk every evening; but that she would not be able to give him any more. The poor woman said she was very sorry, but that she hoped Charley might now get along without it.

After they left the house, John's mother did not say any thing to him about the sick boy and the milk. She saw that John was thinking, and she thought it was better to leave him to make his own conclusions.

That night when they sat down to supper again, little John found his bowl of milk by his plate, as usual. But he did not seem as if he wanted to eat; and after some hesitation and confusion, he went up to his mother and whispered in her ear, to know if he might do what he pleased with his milk. His mother gave her consent, and John put on his hat, and took his bowl of milk, and went out.

After some time John came in again, his little face glowing with pleasure. "Oh ! mother," he said, "I thought I would make my supper on *not*-milk to-night, instead of milk; and indeed, mother, *not*-milk is much the best." His mother knew very well what her little boy meant. He had carried his bowl of milk to Charley; and when he saw how delighted the poor, sick boy was, he said it gave him a great deal more pleasure to do without the milk for Charley's sake, than to drink it. And so, for a little jest, he told his mother that he had made his supper on *not*-milk, and that it was a great deal better than milk.

John's mother was highly gratified, when she saw that her little son had learned the luxury of doing good, and had found that it makes a person much happier to be kind than to be selfish.

———

Casabianca.

The boy stood on the burning deck,
  Whence all but him had fled;
The flame that lit the battle's wreck,
  Shone round him o'er the dead.

Yet beautiful and bright he stood,
  As born to rule the storm;
A creature of heroic blood,
  A proud, though childlike form.

The flames rolled on—he would not go
  Without his father's word;
That father, faint in death below,
  His voice no longer heard.

He called aloud;—"Say, father, say
  If yet my task is done!"
He knew not that the chieftain lay
  Unconscious of his son.

"Speak, father!" once again he cried,
  "If I may yet be gone!"
And but the booming shot replied,
  And fast the flames rolled on.

Upon his brow he felt their breath,
  And in his waving hair,

And looked from that lone post of death,
   In still, yet brave despair,—

And shouted but once more aloud,
   " My father ! must I stay ?"
While o'er him fast, through sail and shroud,
   The wreathing fires made way.

They wrapp   the ship in splendor wild ;
   They caught the flag on high,
And streamed above the gallant child,
   Like banners in the sky.

There came a burst of thunder sound :—
   The boy—O, where was he ?
Ask of the winds that far around
   With fragments strewed the sea—

With mast, and helm, and pennon fair,
   That well had borne their part ;
But the noblest thing which perished there,
   Was that young, faithful heart !

[The above lines relate to a boy of thirteen years of age, who
lost his life in the celebrated battle of the Nile. His father was
commander of the Orient, and was killed in the same battle.]

The Little Violet—A Fable.

Once there was a gentleman who made a beautiful garden.
He laid it out in walks, with nice borders, and he had in it
beautiful grass-plats and pools of water.

He then planted in it all kinds of trees and shrubs and
flowers, and had vines and fruits of every description. The
great oak tree cast its deep shade over the lawn, while the
birds built their nests and sung their songs in its branches.
The apple-tree was white with blossoms in the spring, and in
the autumn it was loaded with fruit.

The vines hung thick with luscious grapes, and oranges,
and all kinds of delicious fruits, grew on every side. The
air was filled with the fragrance of the flowers. There were
the myrtle and the lilac, and other flowering shrubs ; and

also beautiful roses, and verbenas, and dahlias, and peonies, and heart's-ease, and hyacinths, and amaranths, and the sweet little violet, and many other flowers.

It was very delightful to the owner of this garden, to visit it. He would stroll along its pleasant walks, or he would sit in its green shades, and listen to the songs of the birds. He would invite his friends to go with him; and they would pluck the luscious fruits, and · admire the beautiful flowers; and they all said they had never before seen so beautiful a garden.

But one morning, when the gentleman went to see his garden, he found everything changed. The leaves of the oak tree were withered, and it no longer gave any shade. The other trees, and the shrubs, were also casting their leaves, and they seemed to be dying. The roses had dropped to pieces, and all the other flowers were faded and dead. The grass too had dried up, and the vines were naked; and everything looked desolate and dreary.

The gentleman was greatly distressed to see what a change had suddenly taken place in his beautiful garden, and he determined to try to find out the cause. So he spoke to the oak tree, and asked what was the reason that its leaves were withered, and its beauty all gone. The oak replied, "I have concluded to be idle, because I feel that I am of very little use in the garden. I bear no fruit except a little acorn, which is so bitter that even the pigs will scarcely eat it. If I was like the apple-tree, I would be willing to bear fruit forever."

The gentleman then asked the apple-tree, why it too had put off its leaves, and seemed to be dead. The apple-tree replied that it was a poor unsightly tree, and not tall and spreading like the oak. It produced a few apples once a year, but what of that? It was of no use in the garden, and it was better for it to be dead than alive.

The gentleman then went from tree to tree, and from flower to flower, and put to them the same question, and they all gave him the same answer. They were all discontented with their lot. Those that bore fruit, wanted to bear flowers; and those that bore flowers, wished to bear fruit. Each said that it was of no advantage to the garden, and it had, therefore, concluded to wither and die.

The good man was deeply afflicted, and walked about with his eyes upon the ground, grieving that his lovely garden

should so suddenly have become a waste. At last, in one
corner of the garden, he saw a little violet growing where
he had planted it, and looking bright and beautiful. It was
the only flower that was blooming in the whole garden; but it
held its little head as high, and its colors were as beautiful,
and its odor as fragrant, as ever.

"How is it, my sweet little flower," said the gentleman,
"that you are bright and happy, while every thing else in
the garden is discontented and withered? I planted the
others in the best places. I put them in my nicest borders,
and along my principal walks; but I placed you in this distant
corner, where few would ever see you. Yet they have de-
serted me, while you are as joyous and beautiful as ever"

The violet replied, "I know, sir, that you would not have
put me in this corner, if you had not wanted me here; and I
am well contented to stay where you think it best to place me.
I know I am but a little violet, and cannot do much; but I
wish to do what little I can, to make your garden beautiful
and pleasant to you. So I determined to be the best little
violet that I could, and to show myself as bright and as
fragrant as possible"

The gentleman was delighted at the good conduct and sweet
temper of the faithful little violet; and so he went back to
the oak-tree, and told it how this little flower, planted away
off in a lonesome corner, had behaved, and what it had said.
The oak became very much ashamed, as indeed it ought to
have been, for it was in the most conspicuous place in the
garden; and so it promised the gentleman it would immediately leave off its idle and discontented ways.

The other trees, and all the shrubs and flowers, felt greatly
ashamed also, when they heard how the little violet had behaved; and they, too, determined to follow its example. So
the trees put forth fresh leaves, and the flowering plants put
on new bloom, and the grass grew green again; and in a little time the garden was as pleasant and beautiful as ever.
And all this was owing to the good example of the little violet.

We must learn from this fable to be contented with our
lot, and to do the best we can in it. Let every little child
determine to be the best boy or girl that is possible. Persons, too, who are in humble position, should not murmur or
repine, but remember that God put them there because he

wanted them there.   By imitating the example of the little
violet, we shall be happy ourselves, and set a good example.

All Nature Attests the Creator.

Hast thou beheld the glorious sun,
Through all the sky his circuit run ;
At rising morn, at closing day,
And when he beamed his noontide ray ?

Say, didst thou e'er attentive view,
The evening cloud, or morning dew ?
Or, after rain, the wat'ry bow,
Rise in the east a beauteous show ?

When darkness had o'erspread the skies,
Hast thou e'er seen the moon arise ;
And, with a mild and placid light,
Shed lustre o'er the face of night ?

Hast thou e'er wandered o'er the plain,
And view'd the fields, and waving grain ;
The flow'ry mead, the leafy grove,
Where all is melody and love ?

Hast thou e'er trod the sandy shore,
And heard the restless ocean roar,
When roused by some tremendous storm,
Its billows roll in dreadful form ?

Hast thou beheld the lightning stream,
Through night's dark gloom, with sudden gleam;
While the bellowing thunder's sound,
Roll'd rattling through the heavens profound ?

Hast thou e'er felt the cutting gale,
The sleety shower, the biting hail ;
Beheld bright snow o'erspread the plains,
The water bound in icy chains ?

Hast thou the various beings seen,
That sport along the valley green ;

That sweetly warble on the spray,
Or wanton in the sunny ray;

That shoot along the briny deep,
Or under ground their dwellings keep;
That through the gloomy forest range,
Or frightful wilds, and deserts strange?

Hast thou the wond'rous scenes survey'd,
That all around thee are display'd;
And hast thou never rais'd thine eyes
To Him who caus'd these scenes to rise?

'Twas God who formed the concave sky,
And all the shining orbs on high;
Who gave the various beings birth,
That people all the spacious earth.

'Tis He that bids the tempest rise,
And rolls the thunder through the skies.
His voice the elements obey:
Through all the earth extends His sway.

His goodness all His creatures share;
But *Man* is His peculiar care:
Then while they all proclaim His praise,
Let *Man* His voice the loudest raise.

A Friend in Need.

George Cornish, a native of London, went to the East In-
dies, where he made a fortune. After many years, he returned to London, and immediately went to the house of his only
brother. He was there informed that his brother was dead,
but that one of his daughters was married, and living near
by.

Mr. Cornish went to see his niece, and was affectionately
received. He found there another of his nieces, who was
also very glad to welcome home her rich, bachelor uncle. But
his brother had three daughters when Mr. Cornish went away

to India; and he now asked the two sisters what had become of little Amelia, the third sister.

"Indeed, sir," said the eldest sister, "we do not know what has become of Amelia. We never talk about her, and we try to forget her. She has disgraced herself by marrying a man beneath her, a drawing-master employed in the family; and it has ended in poverty and wretchedness. Our father rather encouraged the match at first; but he afterwards became hostile. He would do nothing for her, and he made us promise no longer to look upon her as a sister."

"And did you make such a promise?" asked Mr. Cornish, in a tone of surprise and displeasure. "Poor sufferer," continued he; "*I* have made no promise to renounce thee!" So saying, he took up his hat, left the house, and started out immediately to search for the missing sister.

He had a long search before he found her. Mr. Bland, her husband, was poor, and had of late been unfortunate; so that he had been compelled to change his quarters very often. At last Mr. Cornish found where Amelia lived. It was in the third story of a house in a narrow alley. As Mr. Cornish went up the steps, he met two officers coming down; one with a bed upon his shoulders, and the other with a bundle of bedclothes. A woman with a child in her arms, was following them, and he heard her exclaim, "Oh, it is cruel not to leave me *one* bed, for myself and my poor children!"

Mr. Cornish advanced to the woman, and looked earnestly at her. At last he said, "Is this Amelia Cornish?" "That *was* my name," she said. "I am your uncle George," he replied; and he sobbed as if his heart would break. The poor woman fainted, and it was some time before she recovered herself. "Oh, uncle," she exclaimed, "what a situation you see me in!" He replied, "It *is* a situation, indeed, poor forsaken creature! But you have *one* friend left!"

Mr. Bland had become so poor, that he had been unable to pay his last rent; and the officers had come to seize property, in order to get the money. Mr. Cornish immediately paid the debt, and made them bring back the bed and clothing. Mr. Bland, himself, had fallen sick of a fever, and was then in a hospital.

Mrs. Bland told her uncle that her husband had always been very kind to her. He was industrious, and did his best to take care of his family; but he could not always get employment. It made her feel heart-broken when her father and her sisters abandoned her; and when her husband was taken sick, and her present troubles came upon her, she felt as if Heaven had abandoned her too. "But in this hour of our extremest distress, you have been sent for our comfort," she said. "Thank God!" said Mr. Cornish; "and your comfort I will be. Dry up your tears—better days are coming!"

As it was too late to move his niece that day, Mr. Cornish sent them up an abundant supply of nice food, to last them till the next. He then went to the hospital to see Mr. Bland, and told him to cheer up, and that his family should be taken care of. The next day he rented a nice house, handsomely furnished. He then took his niece, with her three children, to a clothing establishment, and made her get a supply of clothing for the whole family, including her husband. He then conducted her to the house he had rented, and told her she was at home. "All I ask," said he, "is that you will let me come to see you now and then."

The poor lady could only express her thanks by a flood of tears. She threw herself at her uncle's feet, but he raised her up, and putting in her hands a purse of gold, left the house. He hastened to the hospital, where he found Mr. Bland almost well. The doctor said that Mr. Cornish's visit the night before, had cured him. That very day, they carried him home in a sedan chair, and under his wife's nursing he was soon entirely restored.

Mr. Cornish remained a steady friend to the family of his niece. He obtained a good situation for Mr. Bland, and never wearied of his kindness to Mrs. Bland and the children. He went to see his other nieces sometimes, but he never could think so well of them again, after he found how they had treated their younger sister.

The Blind Boy and His Sister.

"Dear Mary," said the poor blind boy,
"That little bird sings very long.
Say, do you see him in his joy?
And is he pretty as his song?

"Yes, Edward, yes," replied the maid,
  "I see the bird on yonder tree."
The poor boy sighed, and gently said,
  "Sister, I wish that *I* could see!"

"The flowers, you say, are very fair;
  And bright green leaves are on the trees;
And pretty birds are singing there;
  How beautiful for one who sees!

"Yet I the fragrant flowers can *smell;*
  And I can *feel* the green leaf's shade;
And I can *hear* the notes that swell,
  From those dear birds that God has made.

"So, sister, God to me is kind,
  Though sight, alas! he has not given.
But tell me, are there any blind
  Among the children up in heaven?"

"No, dearest Edward, there all see;
  But why ask me a thing so odd?"
"Oh! Mary, he's so good to me,
  I thought I'd like to look at God."

Ere long disease its hand had laid
  On that dear boy, so meek and mild.
His widowed mother wept and prayed,
  That God would spare her sightless child.

He felt her tears fall on his face,
  And said, "Oh, never weep for me;
I'm going to a bright, bright place,
  Where Mary says I God shall see.

"And you'll be there, dear Mary, too;
  But, mother, when you come up there,
Tell Edward, mother, that 'tis you;
  You know I never saw you here."

He spoke no more, but sweetly smiled,
  Until the final blow was given;
When God took up the poor, blind child,
  And opened first his eyes in Heaven.

7

Christian and Hopeful conducted into Heaven by the Angels.

Now, upon the bank of the river, on the other side, Christian and Hopeful saw two shining men who there waited for them; wherefore, being come up out of the river, they saluted them, saying, "We are ministering spirits, sent forth to minister for those that shall be heirs of salvation." Thus they went along towards the gate.

While they were thus drawing towards the gate, behold a company of the heavenly host came out to meet them; to whom it was said by the other two shining ones, "These are the men that loved our Lord when they were in the world, and that left all for His holy name; and He hath sent us to fetch them, and we have brought them thus far on their desired journey, that they may go in and look their Redeemer in the face with joy." Then the heavenly host gave a great shout, saying, "Blessed are they that are called to the marriage supper of the Lamb."

There came out also at this time, to meet them, several of the king's trumpeters, clothed in white and shining raiment, who, with loud and melodious noises, made even the heavens to echo with their sound. These trumpeters saluted Christian and his fellow, with ten thousand welcomes, from the world; and this they did with shouting and sound of trumpet.

This done, they compassed them round on every side. Some went before, some behind, some on the right hand, and some on the left, as if to guard them through the upper regions, continually sounding as they went, with melodious noise, in notes on high; so that the very sight was, to them that could behold it, as if heaven itself were come down to meet them.

Thus, therefore, they walked on together; and as they walked, ever and anon these trumpeters, even with joyful sound, would, by mixing their music with looks and gestures, still signify to Christian and his brother, how welcome they were into their company, and with what gladness they came to meet them. And now were these two men, as it were, in heaven before they came at it, being swallowed up with the sight of angels, and with hearing their melodious notes.

Here also they had the city itself in view; and they thought they heard all the bells therein to ring, to welcome them thereto; but, above all, the warm and joyful thoughts that they had about their own dwelling there, with such company, and that for ever and ever.   Oh! by what tongue or pen can their glorious joy be expressed!   And thus they came up to the gate.

Now, when they were come up to the gate, there was written over it, in letters of gold, "Blessed are they that do His commandments, that they may have right to the tree of life, and may enter in through the gates, into the city."

Then I saw in my dream, that the shining men bid them call at the gate, which, when they did, some from above looked over the gate: to wit, Enoch, Moses and Elijah, and others, to whom it was said, "These pilgrims are come from the city of Destruction, for the love that they bear to the King of this place."

And then the pilgrims gave in unto them each man his certificate, which they had received in the beginning.   Those, therefore, were carried in to the King, who, when he had read them, said, "Where are the men?"   To whom it was answered, "They are standing without at the gate."   The King then commanded to open the gate, "that the righteous nation that keepeth truth, may enter in."

Now, I saw in my dream, that these two men went in at the gate ; and, lo ! as they entered, they were transfigured; and they had raiment put on that shone like gold.   There were also those who met them with harps and crowns, and gave them to them; the harps to praise withal, and the crowns in token of honor.

Then I heard in my dream, that all the bells in the city rang for joy; and that it was said unto them, "Enter ye into the joy of your Lord."   I also heard the men themselves sing, with a loud voice, "Blessing, honor, glory, and power, be to Him that sitteth upon the throne, and to the Lamb for ever and ever."

Now, just as the gates were opened to let in the men, I looked in after them ; and, behold, the city shone like the sun.   Its streets also were paved with gold, and in them walked many men with crowns on their heads, palms in their hands, and golden harps to sing praises withal.   There were also some that had wings ; and they answered one another without intermission, saying, "Holy, holy, holy, is the Lord."   And after that, they shut up the gates, which, when I had seen, I wished myself among them.

The Dying Christian to his Soul.

Vital spark of heavenly flame !
Quit, O, quit, this mortal frame !
Trembling, hoping, lingering, flying,
O, the pain, the bliss, of dying !
Cease, fond Nature, cease thy strife,
And let me languish into life !

Hark ! they whisper ; angels say,
Sister Spirit, come away !
What is this absorbs me quite—
Steals my senses, shuts my sight,
Drowns my spirit, draws my breath ?—
Tell me, my soul, can this be Death ?

The world recedes,—it disappears !
Heaven opens on my eyes ! my ears
    With sounds seraphic ring !
Lend, lend your wings ! I mount ! I fly !
O Grave ! where is thy victory ?
    O Death ! where is thy sting ?